Survey Research

Survey Research

Report of the Consultative Group
on Survey Research

Social Sciences and Humanities Research Council of Canada

ISBN 0-660-00380-5
Ottawa, 1976

Le texte français est publié sous le titre,
*Enquêtes-sondages : Rapport du Groupe
consultatif sur les enquêtes-sondages*
Conseil des Arts du Canada
ISBN 0-660-00379-1

This report was originally published by
The Canada Council.

It is now available,
without charge, from
Social Sciences and Humanities
Research Council of Canada
P.O. Box 1610
Ottawa, Ontario
K1P 6G4

Contents

Foreword

The Canada Council has been enabled by Parliament and by private benefactors to support a wide variety of research in the social sciences. Helping the Council to review applications for grants has been a large and eminent company of scholars, many as members of the Council's Advisory Academic Panel and many more as assessors of individual research proposals. These advisers have often said that, while they did not wish to see the Council declaring unilaterally what research should be done or how, they could see a part for the Council to play in making it possible for a group of scholars to articulate for their field of study some paths along which research could be pursued more coherently, rationally and productively. In this way the perceptions of their colleagues and of assessors and supporters of research in the field could be re-examined and perhaps sharpened. Over the past year and a half the Council has set up several Consultative Groups to review their own scholarly fields for this purpose.

Substantial scholarly effort has been going into systematic surveys of social behaviour and attitudes, and substantial sums have been put into these surveys by this Council and by others. Accordingly it was decided that one Consultative Group should examine the special problems of survey research in Canada for the consideration of all involved in conducting and using surveys, including those who underwrite the costs. We have been most fortunate that a distinguished and experienced group of researchers agreed to attempt this task.

They are Raymond Breton (Professor of Sociology, University of Toronto) as Chairman of the Group; Jacques Brazeau (Director, Centre for Survey Research, University of Montreal); Léon Dion (Professor of Political Science, Laval University); David Elkins (Professor of Political Science, University of British Columbia); Maurice Pinard (Professor of Sociology, McGill University); Jenny Podoluk (Statistics Canada); Mildred A. Schwartz (Professor of Sociology, University of Illinois at Chicago); Fred Schindeler (Ministry of State for Urban Affairs); and Harry Eastman (Professor of Economics, University of Toronto), observer from the Council's Advisory Academic Panel.

Within their terms of reference, the members of the Group have been free to explore the subject in their own way and to come to their own conclusions. In the following pages they recount their procedure and set out for the reader's consideration the manner in which they see the conduct and support of survey research in Canada being improved. Nothing can be said here that would add to the authority inherent in their work.

It is hoped that this report will generate discussion within the academic community. The Canada Council is studying the recommendations it contains and will be pleased to receive as soon as possible, letters from persons who wish to put forward their ideas or suggestions.

Part Two of the report, on the standardization of socio-demographic data, is intended to provide an intellectual initiative which survey workers in the field may pursue or not as they see fit.

It remains for me, on the Canada Council's behalf, to thank the members of the Consultative Group on Survey Research for their willingness to accept this assignment and for the many hours of work and miles of travel they have undertaken, collectively and individually, in pursuit of their task.

Charles Lussier
Director
The Canada Council

Foreword of the original, 1976, publication

Summary of Findings and Recommendations

To Scholars, Survey Organizations and Granting Bodies

The investigator should consult the granting body well before making formal application for support; the granting body can then say what information will be needed to assess a research grant application.
(p.1.7) Supporting argument will be found on pages indicated.

Both investigator and granting body may prefer a pilot stage grant to test the survey instrument, clarify costs involved and seek out suitable collaborators in a major survey.
(p.1.7)

Granting bodies and learned societies can do much to foster productive collaboration in major survey research undertakings.
(pp.1.8-1.9)

The investigator and the intended survey organization should determine precisely their respective roles and expectations in carrying out the work before applying for a grant, and these details should be set forth in the grant application.
(pp.1.6-1.8 and Appendix A)

When more than one survey organization is capable of carrying out the stipulated work, competitive bids should be received and submitted with the grant application.
(pp.1.7-1.8)

To Governments and Granting Bodies

It is in the interests of governments, as clients for the results of surveys, to provide directly, or through their organizations, investment for supporting research that will enhance the theoretical and methodological capabilities of university survey centres.
(p.1.14)

Given the learning and experience required for leadership in survey research, a scheme of internships should be worked out with university survey centres, the awards to be offered to a few appropriate candidates.
(p.1.10 and Appendix B)

A peculiarly Canadian problem is the development or adaptation of measuring instruments in survey research that

are suited to Canada's varied cultures; applications for support in work of this kind should be assessed on their merits as such.
(pp.1.14-1.15)

The productivity of survey research can be greatly enhanced by well-run major data banks; because these will be useful far beyond the institutions that house them, they should be regarded as regional or national research resources and their development and operating costs should be funded accordingly.
(p.1.21)

The arrangement for deposit of data and the date when they will be released to others should be stated in the grant application and may become conditions of acceptance of the grant.
(p.1.19, pp.1.21-1.22)

Costs of preparing data for useful storage should be indicated in the grant application, although the disbursement of funds for this purpose may occur later as a supplementary grant.
(pp.1.20-1.21,p.1.22)

Investigators should strive for standardization in collection and coding of data to permit inter-survey comparisons, so far as is compatible with the essential purpose and design of the research; if standardization imposes extra cost, it should be an eligible component of the budget on which the research grant is based.
(pp.1.17-1.18 and Part Two)

Principal investigators will often need release from other duties at the beginning and end of major survey projects; stipends for this release should be allowable in research grants and payable as accounted for.
(pp.1.22-1.23)

Grant applications should include minimum stipulation for the protection of survey respondents.
(p.1.26)

Investigators should take care to avoid saturation of those populations that are frequently subjects of surveys.
(pp.1.28-1.29)

Part One

I Introduction

The survey as a tool of social science is valued and used by academic researchers, governments, social and economic institutions and commercial organizations. Scholars use surveys to describe aspects of social reality and to explore theoretical issues in relation to it; policy makers and organizational leaders use them for input into their decision-making; administrators and businessmen use them for the planning and evaluation of programs and activities. The range and frequency of surveys appear to be increasing in Canada, although dependence on them may fluctuate among different kinds of users.

Survey research poses a number of problems for researchers and for the respondents who are asked to collaborate; university survey research also poses problems for granting agencies and their assessors of survey proposals. In view of these problems, the Development Committee of the Canada Council's Advisory Academic Panel invited a number of people involved in non-commercial work of this kind to form a Consultative Group on Survey Research. The task assigned to the Group was:

1)to assess the distinctive status of survey research in Canada, with special attention to ongoing projects such as electoral surveys and longitudinal studies;

2)to make proposals, in the light of past experience, for methods of organization that will ensure the most effective and economical conduct of survey studies in Canada;

3)to review the problems posed by the rapid accumulation of data with a view to specifying guidelines to promote better coordination and cooperation in the fields of data exchange, taking into account the need to ensure accessibility as well as confidentiality of data;

4)to make recommendations on the policy the Canada Council should pursue in survey research, the research objectives to be sought through these studies, the administrative means to employ and the financial assumptions to be made; and

5)to consider the proportion of Canada Council research funds to be devoted to this form of research.

To examine these questions from as many relevant perspectives as possible, several criteria were used in the constitution of the Group: the type of institution involved with surveys (universities, survey centres, government departments); the academic disciplines for which surveys constitute a research tool (sociology, political science and multidisciplinary fields such as urban studies); and the type of role played in the survey research process (researcher, user of survey data, user of survey results, assessor of proposals, and so on).

Fortunately, these criteria were found to overlap to some extent, making it possible to have a Consultative Group of workable size. The Group did not look closely at commercial surveys, although some of what is said in this report may be applicable there. The main reasons for not including them were two. First, they face problems and follow practices significantly different from those of university scholars and research centres; second, much of their work lies beyond the mandate given to the Group and indeed beyond the sphere of the Canada Council.

The Consultative Group held nine meetings, beginning in November 1973; several members assumed individual tasks to expedite the work. It was necessary first to identify issues that arise from the inherent nature of survey research. The term 'survey,' as used in this report, means obtaining information, usually by questionnaire or interview, from a random probability sample of a defined population. This sample may be defined in terms of a geographical boundary, in relation to a locality or by organizational membership; or the population may be identified by specific individual attributes. The sample may consist of persons, groups of persons (e.g., families) or organizations. Survey responses are commonly too numerous to be collected and handled by a single person.

By its very nature, survey research raises a number of problems. To begin with, survey research usually requires some degree of organization. This organization may consist of the researcher assisted by one or two persons, but researchers frequently delegate work to a survey organization. Thus the capabilities of the chosen survey organization and especially the relationship of the researcher with the organization are questions that need to be considered.

In survey research it is difficult to repair mistakes and oversights midway through the work, and so the initial design is crucial. Data collection in surveys has a 'hit-and-run' character: there is no possibility of correcting information by repeated reference to sources of information, as there is for instance in participant observation or the study of documents.

Survey research tends to be expensive, especially the fieldwork of collecting data. The preparatory phase of the survey is of utmost importance, since errors of omission or of commission at that stage may later prove crippling. The costs of data collection, especially in surveys of uncommon phenomena or of recurring events, raise questions about economy through collaboration among researchers, and hence about constraints that collaboration may place on the conduct of the research. Since space in an interview schedule is expensive, the development of measuring instruments especially adapted to this mode of research is another matter of great concern.

By its nature, the survey requires intensive initial investment if it is to give a rich long-term yield. The utility of an expensive set of survey data will depend on how much the data lend themselves to analysis by the original investigator and by others who are given access to the information. If the original survey was carefully done and the results are properly deposited, they can serve many scholars over the years.

Survey research also involves a relationship between researchers and respondents. The ways in which it unfolds bear important implications for both the respondent and the researcher. These implications may include negative effects from the cumulation of survey research activities in a given area: a surveyed population may become uncooperative because they have been disturbed too often.

We have identified a number of issues in survey research. The initial questions, which dictated the agenda of subsequent meetings, are as follows: 1)the current volume of survey research; 2)quality; 3)usefulness of the data for others than the original researcher; 4)actual use of the data; 5)productivity of survey projects; 6)recurring surveys; 7)rights of respondents; 8)saturation of survey populations; 9)survey organizations; 10)secondary analysis; 11)prerogatives and responsibilities of researchers; and 12)social relevance and impact of survey research.

In the course of Group discussions, the issues were somewhat redefined. They were interconnected and regrouped under three major headings which frame this report:

1) the *conduct* of the survey, including its preparatory phase;

2) the *use* of the data not only by the original researchers but also by others who may subsequently find them valuable in relation to their own research interests; and

3) the *people affected* by survey research — researchers, individual respondents and survey populations.

It should be emphasized that the quality of the research and the rights of the respondent were the central concerns underlying our discussion of the issues. Whether the specific matter under consideration was the capabilities of survey organizations, the continuing usefulness of the data or the collaboration of respondents, our fundamental concern was always for the people involved and the quality of the survey research.

The growing reliance on the results of surveys in the formulation and evaluation of policies and programs is more eloquent comment on their social impact and relevance than anything we could say in this report. Whatever purposes the data and analyses are made to serve, whether in the hands of the original investigators and sponsors or ultimately of others, those purposes will be well-served only insofar as the initial survey is well conceived and well conducted. The topic uppermost in the minds of the initiators may indeed have little to do with the questions to which other investigators will later find the survey results applicable in important respects. For this reason we have not presumed to recommend topics that should or should not be explored by survey methods. Nor have we suggested what proportion of the funds of granting agencies should be allocated to survey research. We believe that grantors want to limit their support to survey work of the highest quality, and this means to work to which the investigator is fully committed because he has had a primary part in conceiving and devising it. We welcome the support, by the Canada Council and others, of colloquia in which scholars can agree among themselves on worthwhile directions in research and fruitful collaboration in their pursuit. These may be means to economy of effort and the sharing of valuable assets. Whatever the means, our pre-eminent concern is with the reliability and quality of the survey research to be done.

II Conduct of the Survey

Activities

1. Relationship between the Researcher and the Survey Organization

As mentioned earlier, survey researchers have to delegate some of their work to others and frequently the delegation is to a survey organization. Viewed in this perspective, the survey centre is an organization providing a certain service for a client for a fee. This contractual relationship involves several different aspects, each of which should be carefully considered for its pertinence to the project in question.

On one hand, the researcher needs to know about the standards that will apply, for example, in the recruiting and training of interviewers, the fieldwork and the selection of respondents. On the other hand, the survey organization needs detailed information about the researcher's goals, conceptual design, parameters of the population to be surveyed, type of questions to be asked, and so on. The granting agency and its assessors, finally, should be satisfied that the various relevant points have been cleared before deciding upon support.

Careful negotiations and discussions between the researcher and representatives of the survey organization at the initial stage of a project can have important consequences for the quality of the work and can also save time, avoid errors, and result in better use of resources. Because of this, it was agreed that a document setting out the most important matters that must be considered could be useful to prospective applicants for support in survey research and to their intended survey organizations. Such a document could also be useful to granting agencies and their assessors in pointing out what should be taken into account in deciding on support for survey research.

Accordingly, a set of guidelines is appended; they deal with recommended practice in relation to 1)the research instrument, 2)the intended analysis, 3)the sampling, 4)the fieldwork, 5)the coding, card punching and taping of results and 6)the survey organization in general.[1] The principal investigator is offered in these guidelines a checklist of the matters on which he and his colleagues, and any organization to which important phases of the survey are to be entrusted, should have a clear understanding and demonstrated capability in the parts they are to play. Not all the items listed are necessarily apt to every case; in particular instances, other important questions may arise. These guidelines are meant to assist in the careful planning, preparation and assessment of proposed surveys; they should by no means be taken as the complete and exclusive ingredients of all such planning.

2.Preparatory Phase of the Survey

Given that the typical survey is expensive and that, once the fieldwork is under way, any error in sampling or defect in the survey instrument will be virtually irreparable, the preparatory phase is of paramount importance. In view of this, the following steps are recommended as applicable:

1)There should be consultation with the intended *granting agency* before completion of a detailed application for funding of a major survey.

2)Because the investigator has legitimate demands to make on the *survey organization* and because it has legitimate conditions to impose on him, at an early stage in any major project the fullest possible consultation should take place between the investigator and those in charge of organizing the survey in the field.

3)In a number of instances, the investigator may find it useful or even necessary to have a *pilot stage* for careful testing and perfection of the survey instrument. This may especially apply when his conception has merit but the feasibility of his intended technique is unproven. The pilot stage may involve, in addition to needed theoretical work, some preliminary unstructured interviewing, accumulation of data for designing the sample, drafting and testing the interview schedule, and systematic analysis of the costs that the complete study would entail. Because of this last uncertainty, the pilot stage will often have to be separately funded. As a result the final and much larger appropriation can be based on cost experience for a well-designed sample and workable survey instrument. The pilot phase is also likely to have a beneficial effect on the richness and quality of the ultimate results.

4)Once the definitive specification for conduct of the survey is established, it may be clear that more than one survey organization will be able to carry it out. *Competitive bids* should then be invited, for performance of fully-specified work to given quality standards. These bids should be included with the application for a grant. The guidelines provided with this report are offered for use in inviting and assessing competitive bids for major segments of a survey project.[2] Lump sum bids are not useful unless accompanied by adequate information on the relevant components of the project, as indicated in the guidelines.

3. Collaboration among Survey Researchers

Given the great variety of circumstances met in survey research, there are many in which collaboration among researchers is warranted. Such collaboration may be advisable only for a certain phase of the work or over an agreed span of time. We recognize that those considering working together in any situation have to weigh the trade off between the advantages of collaboration and the advantages of independent endeavours; the latter will include the distinctive rewards for individual achievement in the academic community, progress at one's own pace and avoidance of the extra time and effort entailed in cooperation. Given the expense of survey research, the funding agency has to ask itself whether it should support two projects (or support one and not the other) when it is apparent that as good or better results could be obtained at less cost by combined operations. Some situations justifying collaboration can be illustrated here.

The very scope of the research problem and the variety of talents needed to tackle it may compel an alliance. A collaborative agreement may be essential for the repeated monitoring of phenomena over extended time. The survey that has to be done at specific and perhaps unpredictable points in time (e.g., electoral behaviour or disaster response) may call for another kind of cooperative planning. When a large population is to be scanned at substantial expense to find respondents of an elusive kind (e.g., a specific type of victim), that scanning may at the same time identify other elusive kinds of respondents. Collaboration may be feasible for at least the data collection phase of the survey, which is in any case the most expensive part. The administration of a combined questionnaire to a common sample of respondents still leaves considerable leeway to each investigator in subsequent phases. Collaboration may also reduce the risk of saturating survey populations, a problem discussed at the end of Chapter IV.

Research councils and other bodies offering support to survey research can do much to encourage investigators to enter freely into collaborative relationships at appropriate stages, such as:

1)including a statement in the announcement of the support program that the grantor favours productive collaboration;

2)inviting prospective applicants who make independent preliminary enquiries yet clearly have common intentions to apply jointly;

3)asking external assessors to comment, for the guidance of applicants, when concurrent formal applications imply unwarranted duplication of fieldwork;

4)in very ambitious proposals, offering the applicant a planning grant of which one use would be to develop suitable means for collaboration with others;

5)supporting research planning colloquia which have the exploration and articulation of collaborative undertakings on their agenda;

6)in major long-term survey programs, giving explicit preference where there is some institutional commitment to performance and completion;

7)making adequate announcement of every grant for survey research; and

8)providing in the grant commitment document for deposit and release of collected data by agreed dates, so that others may know the material and use it for their own research or teaching.

Organizations of scholars can also foster useful collaboration in research, for example, by the following means:

9)through bulletins, meetings and other activities that facilitate the sharing of intentions and the discovery of common survey needs;

10)by optimum use of periodic omnibus surveys, to which a few questions can be added at a cost much less than the price of the same information by independent survey; and

11)in survey research centres, by seeking practicable collaborative arrangements during negotiations with clients.

Instrumentality

1.Development of Expertise and Leadership

The quality and productivity of survey research depend on adequate institutional facilities and careful planning of each phase of the survey. But, above all, quality depends on the expertise of the investigators. The qualification of people in the skills required for survey research should therefore be given special consideration. University teaching programs in research methodology perform a substantial part of this task. However, most existing teaching programs involve limited operational experience with survey research. As a result, there are relatively few people who are prepared to assume the responsibility for a major survey project.

The usual research fellowship or post-doctoral scholarship does not adequately meet the need of the able post-doctoral candidate to gain operational experience in all the phases of a survey project. Problems arise both in the financial terms and in the institutional arrangements open to the candidate in search of this experience. Accordingly, the Consultative Group recommended to the Commission on Graduate Studies in the Humanities and the Social Sciences (appointed by the Canada Council in 1974) the provision of awards for internships in survey research institutions, both for the development of needed Canadian leaders in the field and for realization of the academic and public resource potential inherent in the centres themselves.[3] However, a program to assist internships in university survey research centres should be consistent with prevalent and equitable funding arrangements in other fields of scholarly activity.

In brief, we believe that the teaching function of survey centres should be strengthened and expanded. The centres should have a dynamic role not only in training survey research workers but also in the formation of persons who will be able to assume leadership roles.

2.Capabilities and Predicament of University Survey Organizations

In examining the role of organizations in survey research, the Group made initial enquiries of a few commercial survey firms and university survey centres. These showed that the majority of surveys are carried out in Canada by commercial survey organizations. Some are conducted by government agencies. However, university survey centres have a number of characteristics that point up their particular predicament and capabilities. First, their objectives and activities are partly different from those of commercial firms; there are correspondingly different expectations for their performance, to be discussed below. Second, it seems likely that a commercial survey firm will seek to apply its discoveries for the benefit of its own competitive position vis-à-vis other firms, whereas a university centre will diffuse its research results and its advances in theory and technique of research, both through publications and through teaching. Third, the two types of organizations appear to engage in different kinds of research for somewhat different kinds of clients. Most surveys conducted by commercial survey organizations are local or regional in scope and are made in behalf of private enterprises. On the other hand, it appears that most of the money value of survey work done by university centres is for governments or university researchers; nearly half of that work is provincial or national in scope. University centres are more publicly oriented both in their clientele and in the diffusion of the results of their activities.

a. Services Provided by University Survey Centres

The services expected from university survey centres can be subsumed under four headings: research, development, training and data dissemination. We say 'expected' because existing centres do not appear to have the resources needed to provide desired levels of services in all these areas. Yet the provision of such services is part of their self-defined objectives as well as of what is expected of them.

The research services range from the complete execution of a study to the execution of a specific task. In some instances, a centre is asked to design the study, the interview schedule and the sample; to collect and code the data, and proceed to the technical processing; finally, to analyze the data and prepare a report. In other instances, its services may be requested for the collection of the data only or for any combination of the various phases of a survey project. The services of a centre may also consist of technical advice to a researcher about the design of his interview schedule, his sample or any other aspect of his research.

In the kinds of research services offered, university survey centres do not differ markedly from commercial survey firms: the latter will also provide the above services if requested by clients. However, as will be seen, university centres appear to operate within a somewhat different set of conditions.

Development is another important aspect of the role of university centres. This involves work in the theory of measurement as applied to survey research, as well as the development of techniques for various survey research operations. A significant part of this development consists of the formulation and testing of measures that have validity and reliability within the Canadian context — a context that is highly differentiated along such dimensions as region and language.

In addition to measurement, work needs to be done on sampling and the estimation of error with particular sample designs. Developmental work in methods of analysis is also needed. Such developmental work is already carried out, but not to the extent that it should be. We believe it is important to stimulate this work; survey researchers in Canada cannot rely wholly on external sources for advances in this domain.

Commercial survey firms carry out their own developmental work but normally for their own use. In contrast, developmental work in university centres is available to the entire research community.

University centres also have a teaching role. Survey research, whether conducted in universities (in or out of university survey centres), in commercial firms, in government departments or agencies, or in other organizations, requires people who have mastered the necessary skills. Again, university centres perform this role for the entire survey research community and not only for their own requirements.[4]

Finally, the safekeeping of useful data and the management of their accessibility for research endeavours beyond the original objective is another important responsibility of university centres.[5]

b. Predicament of University Survey Centres

The predicament of university survey centres stems from conditions related to their financing and to certain characteristics of their research goals. First, it seems clear that all the services described above cannot be performed at an adequate level from the revenues of research contracts alone. Even if some of the contracts generated profits, the sums involved would be quite insufficient to support a data bank and the costs of development and teaching. In fact, few of the contracts bring in substantial profits. Moreover, the number of contracts is not very large, in the sense that there are periods of fairly low activity.

Up to now, university survey centres have received most of their financial support from the budget of the university with which they are affiliated.[6] This support has been valuable but insufficient to meet their needs. Nor should it be, for the services provided by the centres extend well beyond the host university: the domain of the centres is at least regional, if not national. Because of this, the amount of support that can be expected from the host university will tend to be limited, especially at a time when universities have to operate under more and more stringent financial conditions.

A number of related problems stem from the nature of university research objectives. For instance, university centres may be unwilling to do routine commercial research. This is an entirely legitimate exclusion that serves, in part, to define the very character of their survey organizations. In fact, most people would probably find it inappropriate for university centres to undertake such research. Such a policy, however, means that slack periods in their basic work are unlikely to be 'filled in' by the routine contracts that might swell their revenues.

Second, university centres do not accept contracts that include a secrecy clause: they define the results of their research as destined for the public domain. Again, this is essential to the character of the organization. But it does exclude a potential source of revenue.

Finally, because of their public service orientation, university centres sometimes undertake a project, because of its community interest, at cost or even at the risk of a slight deficit.

We believe that the functions of university survey centres are crucial for the health of survey research and that these Canadian centres should be enabled to perform all their functions at a satisfactory level. Our enquiries show clearly that in their present circumstances they cannot do what is expected of them.

Of course, university centres, as any other organization, must be constantly preoccupied with the efficiency of their operations. Improvements in this direction are certainly possible, but operating economies will hardly be sufficient to meet the costs of their functions and services. Public support appears essential.

Canadians are quite familiar with the arguments for investment by the federal government in facilities for the advancement of oceanography or nuclear physics or astronomy. Analogous argument justifies federal investment at a limited number of points where the means for systematic knowledge of our society can best be developed. (It may be that modest help in the improvement of surveys will be forthcoming under the terms of the Negotiated Grants now being offered by the Canada Council; but this help will be incidental to the purposes of a given research program and can last for only a limited time.)

Government at every level is coming to rely increasingly on sophisticated scanning of populations affected by social change or legislative intervention. Governments therefore need basic theoretical and methodological soundness in the surveys they use. Public bodies that call for surveys will find it is in their own long-term interest to contribute to the development of theory and method that is undertaken by university centres for survey research. Governments may choose to make these contributions through survey contracts or through bodies granting funds for research. In any event, the Canada Council should remain aware of the possible needs of survey research institutions for public financing.

3.Development of Measuring Instruments

A considerable amount of work is needed to develop new instruments for the measurement of concepts, to adapt existing instruments to survey research and to test the validity of existing measures within the Canadian context. Concerning the last, the importance of taking into account the regional, cultural and social variations in our society cannot be overemphasized; nor can the problem of developing comparable measuring instruments in more than one language.

Much of this work must be undertaken by researchers in Canada; we cannot count on researchers in other countries to take care of these matters for us. We have insisted on the important role that university survey centres can play in this connection.

But such developmental research should not be considered as the exclusive obligation of the centres. We wish to encourage other researchers to consider such work in their own areas of specialization. Funds should be provided by the Canada Council and other granting bodies for this essential kind of methodological work, without undue regard to its immediate application and social impact.

III Use of the Data

There are two categories of users of data from a survey project: the researchers who designed the study for a certain purpose and those who subsequently make use of data collected by other researchers. The two types of uses are referred to as primary and secondary analysis. The productive use of survey data in these two types of analysis raises a number of problems concerning the characteristics of the data, their storage, accessibility and manipulation.

One set of issues about both primary and secondary use has to do with the comparability of the data across surveys. Another, mainly in the interest of secondary analysis, pertains to the circumstances and procedures for release of the data. Questions can also be raised about preparation of the data for storage, the attachment to deposited data of the information necessary for efficient re-use and the funding of the operations entailed by efficient deposit and retrieval. Finally, certain conditions can facilitate more extensive analyses of survey data, especially by the primary investigators.

Comparability among Surveys

Comparable data from different surveys at different times and from different populations would enhance the richness of the analyses carried out and increase the productivity of survey research as such data accumulate. Comparability involves the instrument used to obtain the data, the categories used in coding and the units from which the respondents are sampled.

Comparability of responses has usually been discussed from two points of view: problems of translation of questionnaires from one language to another, and problems of 'cross-cultural meaning.' In both cases, the usual assumption has been that similar studies, conducted in different parts of the world, pose obstacles to comparability of responses. The comparison of studies from different time periods or from different parts of the same country can pose the same difficulties. In any inter-survey comparison it may be found that the information obtained and the schemes for coding it may be quite different.

In the study of this question, the Consultative Group decided to have an inventory made of the questionnaires and code books used in a substantial number of major Canadian surveys, to assess the extent to which comparable data already exist and what further developments in this direction it is reasonable to expect. The inventory is not meant to be exhaustive but an attempt was made to include a wide range of disciplines, regions and dates of surveys.[7]

The inventory was meant to deal with questions such as: How much variety is there among Canadian social surveys in the kinds of questions and coding schemes used? What type of question can be easily standardized and what type cannot? This inquiry was restricted to socio-demographic variables, leaving aside for the moment most measures of psychological traits and behaviour. Although the full results of the study of over 100 French and English language surveys may be found in Part Two, a brief summary is appropriate here.

Standardization must remain an elusive goal, but some practices can be improved. Complete comparability is unattainable for at least two reasons: instruments must vary with the purposes of the research; and instruments should be improved over time, even at the cost of exact comparability.

Although considerable variety was evident for almost all questions and coding formats, a great deal more could be accomplished by fairly routine improvements in standardization. For example, nearly all surveys ascertain age or date of birth of respondents, but few code these data by exact year, preferring instead 5- or 10-year intervals. No additional cost is entailed in coding these responses in terms of the year of birth given. Some variables, of course, pose much more serious problems, but even for seemingly intractable items such as occupation or ethnicity it would require only a moderate amount of extra time and money (which funding agencies should be willing to provide) to enhance the value of future surveys for secondary analysis. For example, many surveys lack a separate category for farmers; they should be separate. A standard format for occupations, or at least a flexible and detailed scheme, ought to be acceptable to most academic researchers.

Standardization that gives comparability, or at least compatibility, among coded responses serves the cost-effective goal of secondary analysis. Without too much inconvenience to principal investigators, flexible coding arrangements could encourage the re-use of surveys with double benefits: unit costs would be reduced and greater policy and theoretical relevance attained through the creation of time series and comparative frameworks. We intend that the specific recommendations in Part Two of this report will lead scholars to pursue the goal of standardization. That goal will not be attained informally or 'accidentally'; it will require consistent attention from the relevant scholarly communities.

Concerning the units from which the sample is drawn, it seems that, generally, results of surveys in Canada will be more widely useful for comparative purposes if the sample frame is constructed on the basis of some unit used in the Census. The specific objectives and circumstances of a given survey are, of course, the primary consideration in the design of the sample.

At this point, a word of caution appears in order. It should be emphasized that while comparability is highly desirable to increase the productivity of survey research, there can be reasons for departure. Insistence on uniformity in the questions asked, in the coding of the responses, and in the sample frame for the sake of comparability should not stifle creativity and, as a result, prevent the emergence of new ideas and better ways of collecting survey data. The objective of this report is to encourage researchers to pay attention to the possible usefulness that their data could have beyond their immediate use, and thus to avoid purposeless variation. It is not at all the intention to advocate uniformity that would disregard the deliberate particularities of a specific research problem or foreclose originality.

Release of Data and Storage for Subsequent Use

Three aspects of this question have been considered: the obligation and prerogative of the principal investigator, the provision of adequate and easily communicated information on the data, and the funding of the operations involved.

1. Obligations of the Investigator as Trustee of Expensive Social Data

The social scientist who obtains information from great numbers of informants has in his hands a social asset not easily reproduced. In this sense, he is to a degree a trustee of the data. At the same time, the investigator may have the rights of an inventor in the concepts and hypotheses that led to the gathering of data, and also to findings that result from manipulating the data in unusual ways. If the investigator has overt responses to a recurring event (e.g., voting behaviour) or has done a replication in time or place of a survey already published, his right to withhold data from others may be much less than when the data relate to an original, perhaps speculative or interpretive, theory of behaviour.

Although the scholar must be the first judge, he is not the only judge of when in the future his right to retain survey data will be overcome by his responsibility to release them. The decision on this question should form a part of his initial understanding with the assessors and supporters of his work. We suggest that two years after the data are gathered is as long as they normally need to be held by the original investigator. We appreciate that he can, of course, often release them sooner, and that the length of time he may want to withhold them will depend on the portion of his time devoted to them; this is a question which will be discussed later in this report. The scholar may find good reason, as he proceeds, to want to delay the agreed data release date; the onus is then on him to persuade the other parties to the initial understanding. His colleagues and financial supporters will usually be found amenable to his reasoned request.

The prerogatives and obligations of the researcher for the data may vary with the nature of the study. The more a survey involves replication or quasi-replication of studies carried out previously or in different contexts, the quicker one may expect the release of the data. In some instances, they could be released as soon as they are ready for analysis. On the other hand, the more a survey involves originality, either in the kinds of data collected or in their measurement, the more the researcher can be expected to want to take the time to pursue his own analysis before releasing the data. The problem in such instances can be alleviated by a partial release of the data; that is, a release of those parts of the data which, in the researcher's view, do not incorporate his original thinking.

2. Providing the Information Required for Efficient and Proper Re-use

In general, the re-user of data should have access to the information the original researcher had about pretests, procedures for the actual selection of respondents and circumstances affecting the actual interviews.

Insofar as it is possible, it appears advisable to code and include on the respondent's record those factors that might affect the validity of the data in the hands of other users. These factors may include the characteristics of the interviewers and features of the interview situation: language competence of interviewers and respondents, sharp differences of class or culture between the interviewee and interviewer, proxy informant (e.g., wife responding for husband), economic or other pressing preoccupations of the surveyed population, and the like. This practice preserves with the data some key information on the circumstances of their collection; it also makes possible the study of the effects of given circumstances on the quality of survey data.

The code books should also specify what weighting factor, if any, was used in sampling and, of course, include detailed descriptions of the operations that intervened between the raw data and the coded responses.

The main reason for providing information on the data collection and the subsequent handling of the raw data is to guarantee the most appropriate and efficient use of data by researchers who were not involved in the collection and collation phases of the survey. Clearly, the original investigator and the depository will have to make professional judgments about the information that is to accompany the data.

In special cases, the scholar may decide to preserve the uncoded responses to some questions by recording them into the respondent's tape record. In other cases, the decision may be to preserve the interview schedules themselves (with identification removed) for a limited time, to enable other scholars to process the responses to particular questions in different ways.

3.Funding the Preparation of Data for Storage

A cost is encountered between the completion of the original investigation and the time when the data will be available for a nominal fee to prospective re-users. Survey budgets should in principle anticipate and provide for this sequel to the actual investigation contemplated, i.e., the cost of cleaning, readying and standardizing the deposit for the use of others. This work can be done only with the consent of the original researchers, assuming that respondents were advised of this possiblity at the time they consented to respond.[8] Deposit of data may also require the consent of an institution (school, hospital, prison, etc.) through whose cooperation the survey was conducted. Preparing data for deposit is to be regarded as a task separate from the original survey; it will often have to be funded as a separate operation, at the joint request of the researcher and the prospective depository. Cleaning of data should begin as soon as possible after the data are collected, thus taking advantage of the presence of the researchers and of fresh memories of idiosyncrasies in the data. Early processing for deposit will minimize subsequent costs. Indeed the initial preparation of the data should be done not only for immediate use but also in view of ultimate storage in a data bank.

On the source of funding for this operation, it is our view that deposits of survey data to be made available to scholars at a nominal fee will thus become public assets. Therefore the costs of developing these assets can appropriately be covered by the agency which funded the original survey whether by grant or contract, rather than being a burden on the individual institution in which the data bank happens to be located.

It follows from this, and we accordingly recommend, that university data banks which are willing to receive and file data deposits from survey research, and are willing to make them readily available to other researchers, should be regarded as research resources whose value extends far beyond their own university. We recommend further that these university data banks should be accorded financial support over and above their share of the university funding that follows the conventional formulae.

In view of the above considerations, prospective applicants for survey research grants should be fully briefed on the deposit, storage and release of survey data. They should be informed about the questions in this regard that they will be expected to satisfy at the time of application and about which they will be expected to state their specific intentions. They should be told that assessors of their application will take these intentions into account:

1)Arrangements should be considered at the outset so that data collected in the survey will be available for re-use by other investigators. Before making formal application, the applicant should confer with those in charge of the chosen data deposit on technical features that can make the data more useful to others without jeopardizing their utility for the original purpose.

2)In the formal application for a research grant, the applicant can then indicate:

a)where the data will be deposited for others, including depository's letter of acceptance in principle;

b)by what date (usually not more than two years after completion of the data collection) the release of data is intended (data may be deposited while other stages of the project, such as analysis, are being carried on);

c)what understanding exists with the data depository about re-use of the data, and how this understanding may affect understandings made with informants;

d)that the ultimate deposit should include copies of questionnaires, any field information about locality or characteristics of the surveyed population that might affect the results, code books, etc.;

e)what allowance should be made for a supplementary application to meet the costs of preparation for data deposit (as distinct from data processing in the original project and from the costs of continuing storage), it being understood that this supplementary application will be filed after the data are successfully collected and will cover the depository's costs in making the data acceptable for safekeeping and for use by other scholars at a nominal fee;

f)that the scholar understands the grounds on which the granting agency will consider a subsequent application from him to change the date of deposit.

It is suggested that this information should be included in a special supplement to the Canada Council's *Guide to Applicants for Research Grants.*

Increasing the Output of Survey Research

Because survey research is usually a large-scale operation in both the collection and processing of great quantities of data, the Consultative Group believes that support of major survey research undertakings should include substantial allowances for the time of the principal investigator and for the ancillary costs encountered during the project. This support is especially important to improve the quality of the initial theoretical and methodological work, as well as the analysis and presentation of the research results. This support, as well as improving the quality of the analysis, should shorten the time between the collection of the data and the publication of results; it should increase the volume of analysis that will be published. The productivity and usefulness of surveys, especially with reduced publication delays, would thus be improved.

Requests for such support should, of course, provide special elaboration of the projected timetable and budget, including details on the stages of conception of the survey, analysis and writing of results. The investigators should be prepared to detail what they propose to do with the time during which they would be released from other duties; assessors should be asked to comment on the realism of these intentions. Investigators should also be asked to submit the product of their labours at the conclusion of each major span of released time.

IV The People Affected

The treatment of survey respondents is an important matter from the point of view of both the rights and prerogatives of the persons involved, and the quality and completeness of the responses obtained. There is a contract, often implicit or unwritten, between researcher and respondent. What are the basic understandings of this contract? Should they be made more explicit?

The unwritten contract with respondents involves obligations on the part of the researcher — obligations that go beyond the interview situation itself. For example, the researcher has the responsibility of protecting the confidentiality of the data according to terms agreed upon with the respondent. On the other hand, the exercise of such a responsibility presupposes certain rights of the researcher: he can protect the information obtained from respondents no better than he is himself protected in safeguarding it. The rights of respondents and researchers are in some ways closely tied together.

The treatment of survey populations, as distinct from individual persons, is another important aspect of the relationship between researchers and respondents which also has relevance for the quality and completeness of survey results. Certain segments of the population run the risk of becoming over-interviewed, because they can provide data on research issues that seem important in relation to topical social problems, and because these groups of people are relatively small. There is a level of tolerance in exposure to scrutiny by researchers; requests for information beyond that level are intolerable. In other words, research faces a problem of saturation of overworked survey populations.

A survey research project or a body of survey research can also have an impact on the community. Survey results frequently have audiences beyond the circle of specialists involved in the given area of research. The results have a possible audience of administrators, policy-makers and the public at large, or influential segments of it. Moreover, a surveyed public may be a target as well as an audience for the research, in the sense that results can affect decisions that will eventually impinge on the situation of that population. The social impact of research is tied to the uses of the data not only by the original investigator but also by subsequent users of the raw data or of the investigator's results.

The Rights of Respondents and Related Rights of Researchers

People have a right to privacy; that is, they have a right to accept or reject intrusions into the private domains of their lives. If people agree to reveal personal information to a researcher, it is usually under an implicit agreement of confidentiality, unless there is an express statement by the interviewer to the contrary. Thus, respondents have a right to expect that the confidentiality of the information will be protected. Confidentiality means that the name of the respondent will be removed from the information, so that it will not be possible for users of the information to identify any of its sources.

The right to privacy implies that the consent of the respondent, his parents or guardian (in the case of minors), the institution in which he is interviewed (e.g., school, hospital, prison), must be obtained and that this consent must be based on adequate and true information about the study. The prospective respondent is entitled to an explanation of the purpose of the study, by letter or at the outset of the interview. Admittedly, the circumstances of the initial encounter with the prospective respondent require that the explanation be short and simple. But enough information to enable the respondent to base his consent must be provided. The respondent may make a useful contribution even when he exercises his freedom to refuse to answer a particular question on grounds of privacy.[9]

Once the data have been collected, the information given in confidence must continue to be protected. This care must be exercised in the initial study based on the data, and it must be so in subsequent uses of the data. Researchers must be scrupulous, in the presentation of their results, not to reveal the identity of their respondents or their parents or affected institutions (except with their consent). Survey researchers may have some proprietary rights in unusual combinations of response, even without names, because such combinations may readily reveal the respondent's identity; there is an obligation on the researcher-depositor to eliminate this possiblity. Also, for economy of survey effort and scientific comparability of results, survey responses may often be turned over to central depositories, for reasons set out in Chapter III. These deposits should also be designed to eliminate the chance that any individual respondent can be identified by third parties. Finally, scholars who have conducted surveys (e.g., on deviant behaviour) may have to be safeguarded from compulsion (e.g., by a law officer) to disclose information given by respondents in confidence.

Many procedural questions thus arise in the support of survey research concerning: what the researcher has to say to respondents about his purpose and sponsorship, evidence of the respondent's knowing consent to give information; steps to protect informant and researcher from legal action, undertakings given about anonymity and subsequent control and use of collected data, obligation to report back to subjects on results obtained from analysis of responses, ultimate intention to turn anonymous responses over to a data despository, and conditions that will govern the access to responses by others than the original researcher and respondent.

The ways in which, and the rigour with which, these various kinds of safeguards can be applied depend a great deal on the circumstances governing specific surveys. Because of this, it is difficult to set out precise and general codes to be followed.

Serious consideration should however be given to the questions of privacy and confidentiality in preparing and assessing research proposals. Applicants, assessors, grantors and others preparing or scrutinizing research proposals should be reminded that to put their name and support behind the undertaking means to take a degree of responsibility to be fair to both the subjects of research and the investigators. (In passing, the Consultative Group noted that the Canada Council's new Negotiated Grants and General Research Grants to universities will cultivate within each university its own machinery for examining research proposals made by faculty members in the social sciences.) The proposed supplementary guidelines for survey research (Appendix A) should as a minimum indicate, for applicants and assessors, that in addition to methodology the project will be judged on these factors:

1)subjects' knowledge of and consent to the aim of the project and the use of their responses therefor;

2)privacy of respondents and confidentiality of responses to be safeguarded; and

3)prior understanding in principle with respondents about ultimate deposit and possible re-uses of data.[10]

It is also suggested that prospective respondents be informed about the purpose and sponsorship of the study, and be given assurance about the confidentiality of the information collected in some such form as:

'Our purpose in asking you these questions is (to be filled in for each case). The answers with any identifying information connected with them will be seen only by (the number and status of the few, if any, individuals who must know for the success of the project). Your name will then be removed from the information you give, so that for all other purposes this information is anonymous. The whole set of anonymous answers, as given by you and many other informants, is to be deposited in (name of survey centre) for scientific use by other researchers; this may save you the bother of answering the same questions over again at some later date.'

Finally, the analysis and storage of the data or the transmission of the data to anyone else by the original investigator must be done in such a way that the identity of the respondents is not revealed. Transmission of data in identifiable form can be done only with the informed and explicit written consent of the respondent.

The requirements of privacy and confidentiality in the researcher-respondent relationship must be given serious consideration. That these requirements be met satisfactorily is important for human rights reasons and for future success in survey research in particular, and in social science research in general. Considerable reliance must be placed on the survey research organization as well as on the personal commitment of researchers to the highest possible standards in this regard.

The Saturation of Survey Populations

A saturated survey population is one which has been exposed to extensive interviewing or to undesirable practices associated with interviewing (see below) to the point where resistance to future collaboration by prospective respondents is significantly above the level that would normally be expected. It is the long run interests of the surveyed populations and of survey research which are at stake here, rather than the interests involved in a particular survey. Excessive exposure to data collectors or exposure to questionable practices is likely to reduce the willingness to collaborate with researchers. This is perfectly understandable. The refusal to participate is indeed the only practical means available to most people to protect themselves against too frequent or otherwise undesirable intrusions into their personal, social or organizational lives.

The experience of the Group suggests that resistance to surveys is already growing, in reaction to factors such as:

1)unnecessary or avoidable over-exploitation of a limited respondent population or sample-frame or sampling technique (including over-exploitation of particular occupational or institutional categories such as municipal councillors, tribal elders, school principals, public health nurses, or such segments of the population as ethnic neighbourhoods);

2)accidental overlaps when investigators independently select respondents from the same vicinities or population groups;

3)unsuitable use of surveys so that many are bothered to find a few elusive cases;

4)excessive use of field surveys to train beginners in survey methods, especially if these surveys involve frequently interviewed subjects;

5)abuse of the survey as a disguise for an acceptability test or sales campaign, or even for less legitimate prying; and

6)mystification, lack of briefing of respondents before the survey and lack of information about findings and analytical meaning afterwards.

These practices tend to limit the opportunities for conduct of needed surveys and to degrade the rate and quality of responses obtainable. A number of remedies are suggested both for design practice and field technique:

1)avoid choosing respondents among a population not essential to the particular survey design but known to be essential to many others (Inuit or Indian communities, residents of areas designated for redevelopment, etc.);

2)share sample frame and sampling methods, conform with good practice of survey centres (e.g., that any address when used for a survey is excluded from subsequent samples for a specified period);

3)increase secondary analysis of data already collected;
4)use preparatory letters to respondents to establish the
aims and good faith of the investigators and to show how
interviewers will identify themselves;

5)notify the local press and appropriate local authorities
on the same points before interviewers go into the field;

6)minimize the use of field surveys in introductory social
science courses; maximize secondary use of good data sets
that are readily available; and

7)consider offering some material compensation to respondents in recognition of the time and effort they are
asked to give.

V Conclusions

This report identifies several problems encountered in survey research. There are problems in the scale of operation involved, which usually require some degree of organization. Organization means delegation and the associated problems of quality control. Moreover, the scale of survey research, which is frequently quite large, entails the considerable costs of data collection. There are also problems in the development of measuring instruments that would be valid in particular contexts and yet offer as much comparability as possible. The report covers problems associated with use of the data, their release to others than the original investigator and their storage for future access. It also gives attention to the question of the productivity of survey research projects, to the issue of the protection of actual and potential survey respondents, and so on.

In addition to identifying problems, the report points to the kinds of resources that are needed to cope with them and thus improve the quality of survey research while safeguarding the rights of those involved in it.

Some of these resources pertain to qualified personnel, some to the data, some to the organizational setting, and some to the population of prospective respondents. But the most important of the required resources is qualified personnel. The appropriateness and effectiveness of the survey research organization is vital, the collaboration of respondents is essential, the sophistication of the instruments for data collection and analysis is important; but it is a truism worth repeating that none of these resources has much value without the availability of expertise.

In discussing issues pertaining to the development of expertise, we emphasize the need for personnel capable of assuming a leadership role in survey projects and in survey organizations. And, with a view to making better use of the personnel involved in survey research, we urge that investigators be able to devote blocks of time free from other responsibilities at critical points in a project, such as the launching of data collection and the writing of results. This would increase the productivity of survey projects.

Data collected in surveys constitute valuable public resources. Their ultimate value depends not only on the quality of the original measuring instruments and on their applicability in different contexts, but also on the comparability of the data with other collections and their accessibility to other investigators.

Considerable attention has been given by the Consultative Group to the organizational resources required for the conduct of projects and for the developmental work necessary to master theoretical and operational problems encountered in survey research. The need for organized facilities to make data available to researchers working in different locations and in subsequent periods of time was also indicated.

The continued goodwill of the populations from whom survey samples are drawn is a resource that needs to be protected. It is indeed an essential one. In this case, the problem is not one of creating or developing a resource, but rather of conserving an existing one against illegitimate, questionable, or excessive use.

The required resources are perhaps not equally crucial; yet they are highly interdependent in their development, use and effectiveness. For example, expertise is required to develop organizational capabilities and the latter are necessary to develop expertise. Also survey research should itself be regarded as a resource requiring adequate investment if it is to maintain and preferably improve the quality and usefulness of its results. The training of personnel, the improvement of measuring instruments, the further development of facilities for the use of data and of other organizational instrumentalities — all these depend to a considerable extent on the availability of financial resources. Talent, ingenuity, collaboration and hard work are required, but these cannot yield substantial results without adequate financial resources.

At various points in this report, we have noted that the present level of funding is inadequate to this or that requirement for high quality surveys. But we also believe that the solution to the various problems discussed is more than a question of money, as our recommendations and suggestions clearly indicate.

In concluding, it should be mentioned that we do not believe we have exhausted the subject. Much more could be done, for example, on the question of the rights of respondents. We have not dealt with the part that commercial survey firms play in survey research and the further

roles they could play. Nor have we addressed the complex
issue of the uses made of surveys and survey results once
they have left the hands of the initial researchers. We
hope, however, that our work will encourage others to
look at survey research and its uses and further analyze
the problems it entails; that the recommendations, guidelines and tools that we present in this report will contribute to the improvement of survey research and its results,
and that researchers will be helped to be more productive
and to improve the quality of their research in whatever
area they happen to be active.

Members of the Consultative Group on Survey Research
The Canada Council

Raymond Breton, Chairman (University of Toronto)
Jacques Brazeau (University of Montreal)
Léon Dion (Laval University)
Harry C. Eastman (University of Toronto)
David Elkins (University of British Columbia)
Maurice Pinard (McGill University)
Jenny R. Podoluk (Statistics Canada)
Fred Schindeler (Ministry of State for Urban Affairs)
Mildred A. Schwartz (University of Illinois)

Alan Armstrong, Secretary (The Canada Council)

VI Notes

1. See Appendix A. We have there put together, for convenience, all our suggestions for pre-determination at the time of application for research support, relating to the survey organization and other matters.

2. See Appendix A.

3. See Appendix B.

4. See pages 1.13-1.14 for further discussion of this question.

5. See Chapter III for a discussion of responsibility for data banks.

6. They point to grants from a private foundation for their establishment and to some continuing provincial support.

7. See Part Two of this report, which was prepared by two scholars and is heartily endorsed by the Group as a whole. We believe that all survey researchers will learn from this study.

8. See the undertaking to respondents suggested in Chapter IV.

9. General questions of the ethics of experiments on human subjects and the right to object to what may be looked upon as personal indignities are being examined by another group for the Canada Council.

10. See discussion on pages 1.20-1.22

VII Appendices

Appendix A
Guidelines for Survey Research
Proposals

At several points in the report of the Consultative Group appointed by the Canada Council to look into problems and prospects in survey research, we have indicated that the nature of these expensive undertakings calls for specific kinds of detail in applications to granting agencies that go beyond those matters which must be included in applications for support to do other types of research.

This Appendix is an attempt to cast in operational language the matters we have pointed to as belonging in supplementary guidelines for those seeking support for survey research, should our advice in this regard be accepted. These supplementary guidelines in no way replace the general rules on eligibility, allowable expenses, schedule of research and the like, which are to be followed by all applicants for research support. Rather the guidelines elaborate, for the major survey research proposal, the extra information to be submitted with any formal grant application. Most granting agencies specify in publications and in application forms what detail they require to judge proposals adequately. For instance, the Canada Council publishes a general *Guide to Applicants for Research Grants*, a brochure on the Killam program, and so forth.

These draft supplementary guidelines deal briefly with the preparatory design stages, steps that will make the data more useful to others, the time for data release, special needs of the principal investigator and protection of respondents' rights. It concludes with a longer section on the prior understanding the investigator should have with whatever organization is to carry out the field interviews; for much of this material we are indebted to Jacqueline Hall of the Centre for Survey Research, University of Montreal.

Preparatory Steps

Given that the typical survey is expensive and that, once the fieldwork is under way, any error in sampling or defect in the survey instrument will be virtually irreparable, the preparatory phase is of paramount importance. In view of this, the following steps are recommended as applicable:

1)There should be consultation with the intended granting agency before completion of a detailed application for funding of a major survey.

2)Because the investigator has legitimate demands to make on the survey organization and it has legitimate conditions to impose on him, at an early stage in any major project the fullest possible consultation should take place between the investigator and those in charge of organizing the survey in the field.

3)In a number of instances, the investigator may find it useful or even necessary to have a pilot stage for careful testing and perfection of the survey instrument. This may especially apply when his conception has merit but the feasibility of his intended technique is unproven. The pilot stage may involve, in addition to needed theoretical work, some preliminary unstructured interviewing, accumulation of data for designing the sample, drafting and testing the interview schedule, and systematic analysis of the costs that the complete study would entail. It may also be the opportunity to seek out suitable collaborators. Because of these uncertainties, the pilot stage will often have to be separately funded. As a result, the final and much larger appropriation can be based on cost experience for a well-designed sample and workable survey instrument. The pilot phase is also likely to have a beneficial effect on the richness and quality of the ultimate results.

Comparability and Standardization

Standardization among surveys that gives comparability, or at least compatibility, among questions and coding systems serves the cost-effective goal of secondary analysis. Without too much inconvenience to principal investigators, flexible coding arrangements could encourage the reuse of surveys with double benefits: unit costs will be reduced and greater policy and theoretical relevance attained, through the creation of time series and comparative frameworks.

Release of Data

Although the scholar must be the first judge of when in the future his right to retain survey data will be overcome by his responsibility to release them, he is not the only judge. The decision on this question will form a part of his initial understanding with the assessors and supporters of his work. Two years after the data are gathered is as long as they will normally be allowed to be held by the original investigator.

In a formal application for a research grant, the applicant should indicate:

1) where the data will be deposited, including depository's letter of acceptance in principle;

2) by what date (usually not more than two years after completion of the data collection) the release of data is intended; (data may be deposited while other stages of the project, such as analysis, are being carried on);

3) that he understands the grounds on which the granting agency will consider a subsequent request from him to change the date of deposit;

4) what understanding there is with the data depository about re-use of the data, and how this understanding may affect understandings made with informants;

5) that the ultimate deposit is to include copies of questionnaires, any field information (about the locality or characteristics of the surveyed population) that might affect the results, code books, etc.;

6) what financial allowance he foresaw as being necessary to meet the cost of preparation for data deposit (as distinct from the costs of continuing storage), it being understood a) that a supplementary application would have to be filed after the data were successfully collected, and b) that the allowance would cover only the depository's costs in making the data acceptable for safekeeping and available for use by other scholars at a nominal fee.

Release Time for Principal Investigator

Because survey research is usually a large-scale operation in both the collection and processing of great quantities of data, the support of major survey research undertakings may include allowances for the time of the principal investigator and for ancillary costs encountered during the project.

Requests for such support should provide special elaboration of the projected timetable and budget, including details on the stages of conception of the study and results. The investigators should be prepared to describe in detail what they propose to do with the time during which they would be released from other duties, and external assessors will be asked to comment on the realism of these intentions. Investigators will be asked to submit an account of their progress at the conclusion of each major span of released time.

Informing and Protecting Respondents

In addition to the usual criteria the project will be judged by assessors on these factors:

1)subjects' knowledge of and consent to the aim of the project and the use of their responses;

2)provision for privacy of respondents and confidentiality of responses; and

3)prior understanding in principle with respondents about ultimate deposit and possible re-uses of data.

It is suggested that prospective respondents be informed about the purpose and sponsorship of the study, and be given assurance of the confidentiality of the information collected in some such form as:

'Our purpose in asking you these questions is (to be filled in for each case). The answers with any identifying information connected with them will be seen only by (the number and status of the few, if any, individuals who must know for the success of the project). Your name will then be removed from the information you give, so that for all other purposes this information is anonymous. The whole set of anonymous answers, as given by you and many other informants, is to be deposited in (name of survey centre) for scientific use by other researchers; this may save you the bother of answering the same questions over again at some later date.'

Matters for Pre-determination with Survey Organization

In the case of research based on surveys of large numbers of people, the investigator commonly proposes to employ a specialized survey organization under contract. The greater part of the cost of the research is likely to be the reimbursement of that organization.

For this reason, it is suggested that the applicant should have a clear understanding with this chosen survey centre, specifying what it is to do and how the centre is to charge for its services. This understanding should be worked out before the applicant formally requests support, and should form a part of any formal application for a major survey research project.

The Canada Council, for example, submits each Research Grant application to qualified and independent assessors for advice. The Council and its assessors will, in the case of a major survey research proposal, take into account the applicant's responses to the questions noted above and below.

1.Research Instrument

a.Role and Capability of the Survey Organization

What will be the role of the survey organization in constructing the questionnaire(s) or other instrument(s)?

Does the staff of the organization possess the competence and experience necessary for such a role?

Is the organization fully aware of the objectives of the research and the analysis contemplated, so that the instrument(s) they will design and/or pretest will yield the data required?

Will the organization provide a full report on the work it will have accomplished in this phase of the operation?

b.Pretesting

Will the survey organization pretest the instrument adequately?

What use will be made of this pretest: to revise questions, validate scales, review coding, verify response rates, check field costs, other?

If the instrument(s) need(s) to be translated, will it (they) be pretested in the translated version(s) as well?

c.Translation

Has the survey organization access to competent translators familiar with interview techniques?

Will they be translating to their native tongue?

d.Material Presentation

Will the page layout and production of schedules be done by people who know how thereby to help respondents, interviewers and coders?

2.Sampling

a.Role and Capability of the Survey Organization

Is the sample to be built by the survey organization, and if so, does its staff have the qualifications and experience for such work?

Will it meet the scientific requirements of the research?

Will the survey organization provide a detailed report on all sampling operations?

b.Type of Sample
Will the sample be taken at simple random, purposively, or following a procedure which involves both random and purposive selection?

c.Size of Sample
Will the sample as a whole, and each of its sub-sections, yield enough cases or enough responses to each question to permit valid analysis?

d.Representativity
From what source will the sample be taken: voters' lists, telephone directories, office records, other?

Is the source from which the sample will be taken truly inclusive of the population to be studied?

Is the sample source up-to-date, and are its gaps known?

What tests will the sample source undergo before use, and once constructed, to what tests will the sample be subjected?

In the event of failure to obtain a response, what practice is to be followed: substitution, quotas?

e.Comparability
Will the sample be based on Census Enumeration Units or otherwise, to facilitate comparisons with other surveys, past and future?

3.Fieldwork
a.Role and Capability
of the Survey
Organization
What will be the role of the survey organization in this stage of the research, and how will the responsibilities be shared between the principal investigator, the survey organization and sub-contractors, if any?

Does the organization possess the personnel with the experience and qualifications necessary for all aspects of the fieldwork?

Is the organization's network wide and strong enough to cover the geographical area from which respondents will be selected?

Can the organization meet given deadlines?

Will the organization provide a comprehensive report on completion of the fieldwork?

b.Survey Techniques

What techniques are proposed to gather the data: mailed questionnaires, individual interviews at home, work or elsewhere, group interviews, telephone, other?

Will these techniques yield the data required, in quality and quantity?

How does the survey organization propose to present itself to the respondents and, where necessary, to the respondent's employer or community?

What response rate is anticipated, and what procedures are proposed to ensure that a minimum number of responses will be obtained?

c.Personnel

What kinds of interviewers will the organization employ: students, professional interviewers?

Will the interviewers be informed of the subject matter of the survey, and what special preparation or briefing will they get?

Will they have the appropriate competence in the respondents' languages?

d.Supervision of Personnel in the Field

How is the supervisory personnel deployed in the survey territory?

Will the interviewers be able to check readily with supervisors during the survey, if need be?

Can the organization enlarge or replace its field forces, should circumstances require?

e.Costing

How are interviewers to be paid: time or piece-work?

How will the client be billed?

f.Quality Control

Does the organization offer any quality controls, such as re-checking with respondents or scrutiny of completed questionnaires to spot major departures from sample or gaps in the data?

4. Preparation of Data for Analysis

Is its role in the preparation of data for analysis clear from the outset?

a. Role and Capability of the Survey Organization

Will the organization provide a report on this phase of the operation?

b. Coding Plan

Will the coding system provide the information needed for the analysis?

Will the coding system be such as to minimize transcription, maximize pre-coding and facilitate punching of cards?

Will the codes be compatible with the computer and programs which the principal investigator will have at his disposal for analysis?

Who will be responsible for changes in the coding plan, and how are these changes to be standardized among coders?

How will non-responses be coded to make it possible to calculate the deviation from the sample plan?

What procedures will be used to code responses to open-ended questions, and are the people who will be responsible for this operation adequately informed of the objectives of the research?

c. Coding Personnel

How will coders be recruited and trained?

Will the coders be adequately supervised?

Will they possess sufficient competence in the language of the questionnaire?

d. Quality Control of Coding

What checks during coding will be used?

What percentage of errors will be tolerated, and how are errors to be corrected?

e. Punching and Magnetic Tapes

What percentage of error will be tolerated in punching, and what procedures will be used to control the quality of the operation?

In what form will the data be provided to the principal investigator?

If magnetic tapes are used, will they be compatible with the computer devices at the disposal of the principal investigator?

5. Analysis

Will the survey organization be involved in the analysis of the data, and if so, how are responsibilities to be shared between the organization and the principal investigator?

Are the organization's staff, computer programs and equipment adequate for its part in the analysis?

Has the staff of the organization the training and experience to particpate in the elaboration of the scheme of analysis, the construction of analytical tools, or the interpretation of results?

6. The Survey Organization in General

What are the special qualifications and interests of the organization's directors, professional heads, etc.?

What kinds of survey are they accustomed to doing?

a. Role and Capability

Have they the staff, equipment and space to handle the work they would take on?

If the principal investigator is not himself a specialist in survey technique and methodology, is the survey organization willing and able to help him in these matters?

b. Sub-contracting

How much of the survey operation will the organization do itself, and how much will be sub-contracted?

How are sub-contractors to be chosen, and on what basis are they to be reimbursed?

c. Costing

How detailed are the cost estimates provided by the organization?

Will the organization sign a firm contract, or will the final cost be known only when the operation has been completed?

Given the quality demanded, are the estimates both competitive and realistic?

How does the organization estimate its administrative costs: lump sum or percentage?

d. Protection of Respondents

What safeguards are offered for the confidentiality of responses and protection of respondents?

What is the organization's policy on deposit and re-use of raw data or data processed to varying degrees?

e.Bidding

If the vital considerations in the above checklist have been determined in writing and it is quite clear that two or more survey organizations are equally competent in their capabilities and the quality of their performance to conduct the delegated parts of the survey research project, the funding agency may reasonably expect to see competitive bids for the work.

Appendix B
Internships in Survey Research
A Submission to the Commission on Graduate Studies
in the Humanities and the Social Sciences

The Consultative Group on Survey Research is chaired by
Professor Raymond Breton of the University of Toronto
and is composed in addition of the following:Jacques
Brazeau (University of Montreal); Léon Dion (Laval University); David Elkins (University of British Columbia);
Maurice Pinard (McGill University); Jenny Podoluk (Statistics Canada); Fred Schindeler (Ministry of State for
Urban Affairs);and Mildred Schwartz (University of Illinois). We are invited by the Canada Council to consider
the status in this country of survey research; the circumstances affecting the effective conduct, support and use of
this research; and the weight that should be given to work
of this kind in shaping Canada Council programs. By 'survey research' is meant the gathering of information from a
large number of respondents,often indicative of a still
larger population, and usually in forms that prove manage-
able only with the aid of data processing machines.

Internships in Survey Research

During the course of its deliberations over a number of
months, the Consultative Group has come to believe that
the opportunities for social scientists to qualify themselves adequately in survey research methods are limited
in Canada. Yet those so qualified are needed in growing
numbers in the academic, governmental and commercial
communities. What we think is needed is not simply more
elementary courses: these are already being offered in a
number of universities. The need we see is rather for con-
centrated work at an advanced level in academic centres
specializing in the full range of applications of this methodology. Under the following headings, the need for this
new program is spelled out and a proposal is made for
meeting it.

Existing Programs

In recent years a number of our universities have begun to
offer courses in various aspects of survey research, commonly within their departments of sociology. Our impres-
sion is that these are likely to be introductory courses,
touching on many aspects of survey research method; few
specialized courses in sampling and questionnaire design
are offered. The number of teachers at Canadian universities who have both the knowledge and experience neces-

sary to conduct advanced courses is very limited. Further, few graduate programs can afford to offer many specialized courses of this nature. Finally, as in other fields, the available courses do not tend of themselves to equip students to go out and conduct surveys; before they can use the methods with confidence, students need more penetrating understanding than a general course can impart in matters such as sampling, questionnaire design and data analysis. After the theoretical underpinnings are comprehended, some first hand experience under expert supervision is advisable before the candidate presumes to conduct a large project or to teach others the techniques.

The Institute for Behavioural Research at York University has attempted to provide a more comprehensive training in survey research through its summer program. This program is open to graduate students from all disciplines and offers courses in all aspects of survey research and in such related areas as data analysis. However even this program has serious shortcomings. The student can normally take only one full course during one summer, so that it would take a number of years to get the full benefit of the program. Furthermore, time limitations prevent the summer student from gaining enough experience in the gathering or analysis of survey research data.

Thus, while important steps have been taken over the past five or six years to improve these learning opportunities, they are still far from sufficient to meet the present Canadian need.

The Need for Better Qualified Leaders in Survey Research

Increasing use of survey research on the part of academics, commercial enterprises and governments is creating strong demand for professionals qualified in the use of this methodology. This is a country of sub-societies, sub-cultures, in short a social mosaic. The importance of recognizing our variety of circumstances, attitudes and aspirations, and the necessity for care in delineating them, is ever more apparent. Notwithstanding that confidence in survey techniques is growing and that standards of competence are improving, the demand for highly qualified specialists must be expected to grow even faster. Unfortunately, because so few Canadians are equipped to undertake this kind of research, some positions in the field may be filled by poorly qualified people. The experience of our

Consultative Group indicates that there exists already a
need for more professionals who can give leadership in
Canada in this field.

As these needs become more widely recognized, dependence on highly qualified leaders in survey research will
grow; they in turn will need supporting skills which
should not be imparted by persons whose competence is
confined to one contributory skill. We are of the opinion
that these needs can best be satisfied by providing within
the same organizations opportunities for advanced research as well as for apprenticeship in survey research. To
these centres would come social scientists already well
qualified in the traditional substance of their own disciplines. As researchers they would here be able to study
survey methods and techniques in an environment that
would impose the highest theoretical standards while giving first hand clinical experience in the application of
methods. Only in some such way is Canada at all likely to
nourish a breed of future principal investigators and leaders versed in how to meet the practical problems of survey
research while reaping the full benefits of advancing theory.

Existing academic centres lack the resources to prepare
professionals in the manner suggested. Those now employed in existing centres must devote most of their ener-
gies to specialized tasks related to ongoing projects, usually under pressure of time. They have few hours to devote
to the development of expertise across a variety of problem areas. Nor do they have the free time necessary to
develop theoretical underpinnings for survey work. Yet
these centres come nearest to offering the opportunities
and expertise for the educational tasks we are prescribing.

A Proposal for Internships in Survey Research

We are convinced that the solution to this situation is to
provide funds for a few internships at university survey
research centres. These internships would free the social
scientists who hold them from the familiar necessity to
'earn their keep' by performing routine tasks within the
centres or elsewhere. Having already achieved complete
status as scholars, the interns would also be free from com-
peting academic pursuits. From the point of view of the
survey centres, the internship revenues would make possible exploratory association with leading survey profes-

sionals, in ways that cannot be justified either as teaching costs or as contract costs to those coming for survey services. The centre would have to have a voice in setting the number of internships and in choosing the best candidate.

To attain these goals, the internship program should be characterized by the following features:

1)Interns not proceeding to degrees should be eligible for awards; no intern should have concurrent course work obligations;

2)The program should be funded by sources independent of those now accessible for ordinary university operations, in consistency with the view that the survey centre is a regional or national facility, not appertaining merely to the campus where it happens to be situated;

3)The funding of internships should be sufficient to allow stipends for interns, expenses connected with their research and university overheads;

4)Each internship should be of at least one year in length, so that the intern will have enough time to become well founded in the work; but because of the limited number of available places, duration of internships should permit rotation of interns within the accepted time scale of preparation for specialized careers; and

5)Final choice of interns should be made by the funding agencies, from slates of nominations made to the funding agencies by the university centres where the interns would study, in recognition of their respective interests in a fair and workable program.

Conclusion

We believe that the scheme we have outlined would provide interns with required opportunities, otherwise unattainable, for:

1)Development of skills in the methods of survey research

First hand experiences with survey data provide indispensable perspectives and insights that cannot be gained from the literature; at advanced levels this access to and facility with survey materials is the basis of original methodological inquiry.

2)Experience with more than one large-scale study
Students of survey research conventionally have access to

one survey from which to draw dissertation materials; exposure to a variety of kinds of survey, all carried out to high standards, can greatly enrich the mastery that leaders in this field ought to have.

3)Contact with other survey researchers
The essence of the university lies in the face-to-face contact of people with ideas. Mutual respect grows from these encounters, as may friendship; the respect is as necessary to the growth of knowledge as it is to the building of careers. To work with others in a milieu in which the common concern is the advancement of survey research, through the internships we recommend, seems to us necessary to both kinds of advancement and hence to Canadians' understanding of themselves.

Raymond Breton, Chairman
Consultative Group on Survey Research
The Canada Council
December 1974

Part Two

We wish to thank the Canada Council for funds to carry out this research, and the members of its Consultative Group on Survey Research for comments and suggestions. Wendy Thompson, Information Systems Manager, Institute for Behavioural Research, York University, was very helpful in locating some of the studies. A number of researchers were also most generous in providing us with material and other help: Donald E. Blake, Jacques Dofny, Jean A. Laponce, Marc LeBlanc, Vincent Lemieux, Maurice Pinard, Jenny Podoluk, and others. The following served as invaluable research assistants: Roger Lapierre, Grace Skogstad, Ian Stewart, and R. Jeremy Wilson.

The Standardization
of Socio-Demographic Data
in Canadian Social Surveys
by David J. Elkins
University of British Columbia
and Jacqueline Hall
University of Montreal

Report prepared for the
Canada Council Consultative Group
on Survey Research
Ottawa, 1975

I Introduction

A survey is a technique for the collection of standardized data on a relatively large number of cases (usually individuals or households) in which the combinations of values of these standardized variables are 'given' and are not subject to manipulation by the investigator. In this context, standardized means that for any given variable each case is coded according to the same criteria and on the basis of information elicited by the same (or an equivalent) question, item, or observation.[1] This degree of standardization distinguishes survey research from such forms of data gathering as participant observation, clinical diagnosis, depth interviewing and historical reconstruction. Similarly, lack of manipulation in survey research is contrasted with experimental work where random assignment to treatments and control of treatment type and quantity are the hallmarks. Manipulation of treatment is, of course, a matter of degree, and some surveys can perform operations more or less equivalent to laboratory experiments. Nevertheless, the distinction is clear for the variables included in this report, since researchers cannot 'assign' persons to socio-demographic categories such as sex, occupation, ethnicity, religion or political party affiliation.

The purpose of standardization is enhancement of comparison of cases. For many purposes, however, it is important to make comparisons of cases which are not part of the same survey or the same wave of a survey. One can study similar phenomena in different places or at different times if at least some variables have been standardized across places or times. Since the intent of this investigation concerns Canadian research, we may take for granted a degree of common meaning and experience not found in explicitly cross-cultural or cross-national surveys.[2] Even so, questions in different languages or idioms within a Canadian context must be considered carefully for possible biases. This is true not only when comparing Quebec with the rest of Canada; class, ethnic, regional, and generational differences of meaning may also be found. Presumably proper pretests and carefully standardized coding schemes will aid in the identification of potential problems. *We recommend, however, that scholars be familiar with the general literature on cross-cultural equivalence of survey questions, even when no problem is known to exist.*[3]

Since the same investigator is rarely involved in all the surveys one might wish to use, standardization (to the extent it occurs) has been the result of informal communication among researchers or the result of special professional norms about the best or most useful ways of asking questions and coding responses. Such norms, though not applied as frequently as might be wished, are achieving fairly wide recognition in sampling and interviewer conduct; they are not so common as they relate to questions and coding. For example, probability sampling is the generally accepted norm, appropriate stratification and other procedures being introduced according to the particular nature of the target population and the research objectives. In interviewing there are norms about the timing of callbacks, about rapport, and the like. However, many surveys ask questions in different ways and use quite varied coding schemes; in many cases, they do not even ask basic questions. This obviously restricts greatly the potential for secondary analysis of these surveys.

It is only recently, however, that survey practitioners in Canada have concerned themselves with standardization of the survey instrument itself. This report is a first effort in this direction. It cannot pretend to be complete or definitive. It is itself based on a survey of surveys, and is intended to describe in broad terms the extent to which standardization has already occurred and the potential for further standardization by social scientists in Canada. On the basis of these data, we make policy recommendations at several points in the text, and we include sample questions and coding schemes.

Some of the conclusions are applicable in many other countries (for example, those on age, marital status, nativity, and the like), but most are at present peculiar to the social features of a country characterized by regional, linguistic and ethnic diversity, economic and occupational changes, and rapidly changing levels of education and affluence.

II Terms of Reference

Comprehensive analysis of standardization is impossible. One would need years of work simply to enumerate the 'population' of all existent Canadian surveys in the social sciences. These would include academic, commercial and government surveys. Instead we have tried to include surveys which satisfy all or most of the following criteria:[4]

1)Primarily concerned with Canadian social life, where 'social' is conceived broadly to include educational, economic, and political as well as social more strictly construed;

2)Extensive surveys, where extent is measured by geographic coverage, size of sample, range of questions, or theoretical focus. This excludes, for example, surveys of 20 farm families in one community;

3)Different disciplinary backgrounds of the investigators;

4)Different time periods from 1960 to the present day;

5)Different geographic and non-geographic populations — federal, provincial, local, special sub-groups (students, homeowners, etc.), and comparative; and

6)Variety of theoretical focuses — some narrowly focused (hypothesis testing), some descriptive, some virtually omnibus.

Moreover, in view of time and cost constraints, the choice of survey was to some extent dictated by accessibility, and this has resulted in some 'clustering' of the material, the richer sources of survey data having been abundantly drawn upon. In short, while the studies examined do not constitute a random or representative sample, they reflect, we are sure, a wide range of locales, interests, rationales, and time periods. The purpose, after all, is to consider whether consensus exists, and if not how it might be achieved.[5] Therefore, such variety ensures that we are not likely to report consensus where it does not exist, nor are we likely to have omitted radically different procedures for eliciting information or coding it, at least among the types of studies which academic social scientists in Canada are likely to use for secondary analysis or to use as a model for a new survey.

Given these considerations, there are several questions which we have tried to answer in a preliminary fashion.

1)Is there consensus on the inclusion of any given variable? For example, do virtually all studies ask about age, sex, or occupation of respondents?

2)When asked, is there consensus about the format of the questions? Exact wording is not essential, but do studies elicit the same kind of information? For example, do they ask only for age in groups (under 25, 25-45, etc.), or do they elicit age in years?

3)For information elicited, do the surveys code this information or do they 'lose' information? For example, some ask year of birth but code only broad categories.

4)Is there consensus on a coding scheme? If categories are used (as in occupation), are these similar across studies, locales and time periods?

5)Insofar as no consensus exists on the above characteristics, what is the range of variation? Are there two main types of coding schemes, for example, or three or a multitude?

6)Insofar as no consensus exists, how far are variations the results of legitimately different research objectives, population types or data collection methods? Or how far are they the result of inadequate reference to existing studies, or of inability to recognize the re-use potential of data?

7)Most difficult of all, and most tentative of all, what recommendations can one make about question format, question use and coding schemes? In some cases, great variety of usage may reflect haphazard invention on the part of researchers, or even sheer accident, and so mask a potential for standardization or improvement. In others, variation may be justifiable, and standardization would paralyze the development of research. No validity checks have been made for this report, so our recommendations must take the form of hypotheses for investigators using questions in the areas we discuss. *Moreover, what recommendations we make are intended primarily for the researcher who has no particular reason to wish to innovate or experiment with particular variables. Such a researcher will, we believe, benefit from using already tried and tested techniques, and will do service to the research community at large by providing material for comparative analysis.*

The suggested questions and codes given in later sections serve only as a first step towards standardization of socio-demographic variables in Canadian social research. Maximizing the re-use capabilities of data through standardization involves not merely encouraging researchers to use the *same* questions and codes, wherever applicable, but above all determining which are the *best* questions and codes in a given research context, taking into account the differing conceptual and methodological factors which make up such a context, involving repeated experimentation and validity checks which we were not able to undertake in the preparation of this report.

It was thought useful, however, to compile a list of commonly used variable forms for two purposes. First, it would seem reasonable that analysis of the reliability and usefulness of different questions and codes should begin with the forms that are most widely encountered at present and therefore have in their favour the fact that they lend themselves to comparison with existing data; innovation clearly should not be undertaken without due consideration to the weight of comparative potential these forms afford. Second, since the attainment of standardization through concerted testing and innovation would seem to be a long way off, it was felt that the many researchers who will be designing research instruments in the interim could well benefit from the tentative list we have compiled. As we repeatedly note, much of the nonstandardization to be found at present appears to be related less to the wish to perfect existing questions and coding schemes than to a lack of awareness about their existence. By providing in some compact and accessible form the main questions and codes in use at present we may limit the amount of nondirected innovation which occurs, and thereby add to the body of material available for comparative analysis.

It goes without saying that the questions and codes listed below are intended for use as background variables only. Researchers who wish to explore in any detail fields such as language use, religious practice or social mobility, to name but a few, will need to go into considerably greater detail. The following list concerns them, therefore, only insofar as they could usefully try to render their own data compatible with the basic forms. For instance, a researcher who is interested in population migration patterns will want to code more information about successive places of residence than is contained in the questions and codes given here. However, if he is in a position to construct his finer breakdown of 'size of place' in such a way as to respect the same cut-off points as are used in the standard code, his data will be more useful for others who have another purpose in mind.

The codes and questions cited are mainly those used by Statistics Canada, the Survey Research Centre (York University), and the Centre de Sondage (University of Montreal). This choice was made, not on the assumption that what is standard practice in these organizations is in any way automatically better than what is done elsewhere, but simply because besides having accumulated considerable experience, these agencies are prime sources of data for secondary use by academic researchers. In the case of the two university centres, it should be remarked that the variable forms listed are not those used in all the surveys they have undertaken, since the choice is often made by an outside principal investigator and not by the research centre itself. It is likely, moreover, that useful questions and codes not known to the authors of this report have been omitted. It is to be hoped that such omissions will be brought to our attention so that the list may be made more comprehensive.

Coding categories have been listed for most variables but numeric codes are not attributed to them because of the varying requirements in software and hardware that may prevail at different institutions. Nor are missing data codes given, since the inclusion or omission of each of these will depend largely on the structure of the interview schedule. It may, however, be noted that the following missing data categories are normally used whenever relevant, and should not be collapsed:

don't know
(respondent states he does not know the answer to the question)

refuses
(respondent states he does not wish to answer the question)

no answer
(interviewer mistakenly omits the question, or fails to obtain any answer at all)

not applicable
(question is skipped, because the answer to a previous question renders it inappropriate)

The definition of the last category is worthy of attention. The category 'not applicable' should be coded as missing data only when the structure of the interview schedule specifically calls for the question to be skipped, and the reason for the omission is clearly coded elsewhere. Interviewers, respondents and coders should not be at liberty to decide that a question is 'not applicable' for reasons that are not related to specific skip instructions contained in the schedule. If a question is found to be inappropriate for reasons not foreseen in the schedule, a special category explaining the reason should be created and should not be coded as missing data since, by definition, this category will contain information which is not available elsewhere.

III Principles and Values of Standardization

Secondary analysis is one of the primary uses of survey research. Such usage will no doubt increase with time for several reasons. For one thing, as time passes we have a greater time span of previous studies which can be re-analyzed for trend and time comparison. Second, surveys are expensive and re-use reduces the unit cost. Fortunately, it is generally true that extremely expensive surveys are broad-gauged and therefore lend themselves, more than narrower and cheaper ones, to re-use in other contexts. (A possible exception is that of telephone surveys, of which more will be said later.) Third, as our knowledge increases and as theories and hypotheses are propounded, we may think of additional ways of using existing data. This may take the form of complex indicators and scales not thought of previously, as well as the use of existing data to refine concepts and hypotheses for improved measurement and research design in future studies.

To accomplish these aims and to realize the values of secondary analysis, the relevant set of questionnaires must contain a common core of questions. These must be coded in similar ways (or at least so that they permit redefinition later), and the responses and resulting coded data should be as uniform as possible. Obviously, without planning one will rarely find exactly the same question coded in exactly the same way. This report will demonstrate, however, that a degree of uniformity exists for certain types of socio-demographic variables. Furthermore, some of the variation is not completely crippling for the purposes of specific types of secondary analysis. For example, surveys which fail to ascertain ethnicity as such will often be found to ascertain language and religious affiliation. Such variables can clearly not be considered direct substitutes for one another, and thus cross-analysis potential is severely reduced when the same variables are not present in the different data sets used. However, they are related, and the inclusion of at least one variable of the group may well enhance the possibilities of further analysis for purposes of exploration and design. Additionally, some variation may easily be corrected in future studies if certain basic recommendations are followed.[6] For example, one frequently encountered defect is in the coding of numeric variables such as age and number of persons in the household; individual researchers still tend to group responses according to what they perceive to be the needs of their own intended analysis, thus rendering their data unusable to other researchers. Direct coding of all numeric responses (except perhaps income) would easily eliminate such difficulties at little or no extra cost. Other variations are easy to identify but much less easy to remedy. A number of surveys which ask about occupation, for example, do not code the responses beyond what the investigator needs (such as white collar and blue collar); more detailed coding obviously would allow other scholars to make greater use of such a survey.[7] However, in the case of occupation, no universally satisfactory coding scheme exists that would meet both the methodological and the cost requirements of all the studies; and hence precise recommendations, beyond the encouragement to include more detail, are not feasible.

The value of standardization must be weighed against other research needs and circumstances. It will seldom prove reasonable to expect every question and coded response to be constant over time. That would, for one thing, obstruct the development of better phrasing of questions, clarified coding, or additional means of eliciting information. Furthermore, historical changes in society may require different questions or different coding categories. (Desirable standards may occasionally have to be compromised because of the resistance of sponsoring agencies; otherwise the survey may never be carried out.)

These considerations have been incorporated into this study in several ways. We have been concerned with equivalence of response more than with exact wording of questions. We have examined the degree of detail of coding schemes rather than the precise usefulness of one scheme for any given purpose. We have tried to ascertain some of the circumstances under which responses and coding should vary across domains or time. (For example, a survey designed to study one phenomenon, such as language use, must have a format and degree of detail not fully consistent with broadly focused studies, of which language is only a minute fraction of the social phenomena considered.)

Insofar as no common practices now exist, researchers must determine whether uniformity is desirable, under what circumstances, and at what cost (not only in dollars but in foregone innovations). To the extent that uniform practices exist (as they do for certain variables discussed below), we must justify innovations by the degree to which the improvement they offer outweighs the value of continuity and comparability.

In this report, the focus of attention is on the current degree of similarity of responses and coding schemes. We have generally not attempted to pass judgment on the adequacy of the questions or codes where uniformity exists. To do so would require validity and reliability checks beyond the resources of this study.

There are additional considerations which survey specialists must reconcile with attempted standardization. We can only raise these issues, and not resolve them, in this context. First, surveys are enhanced when they can do 'double duty' by lending themselves to comparison with official statistics deriving from censuses, electoral results, and specialized studies by Statistics Canada and other government agencies. Second, such comparisons with other data sources can be further augmented by sampling procedures; for example, the use of census tracts or enumeration areas as primary sampling units is encouraged or, alternatively, in the case of electoral studies, the use of federal or provincial ridings. Third, improved standardization requires better planning and more money. Investigators must examine existing data sets before deciding on final formats for their instrument. At present, coding is the most consistently under-costed phase of most surveys. Detailed coding costs extra, except in rare cases such as age, and this expense must be built into requests to funding agencies and explicitly justified by reference to its benefits for secondary analysis. Equally important, funding agencies must appreciate that the importance of thorough and comprehensive coding of survey materials justifies the expenditure involved.

IV Variables Included in the Report

We have consciously restricted the variables examined in this study to those of a social or demographic sort, omitting all but a few purely behavioural or attitudinal ones. These latter are worthy of study, but that task is even more vexing than the present one and cannot be considered here. In some cases, the line is not clear between socio-demographic variables to be included and the excluded behavioural or attitudinal variables. For example, occupation is clearly socio-demographic, but what about respondent-identified social class or interviewer assessment of class? We have included the latter two variables because they relate closely to the former and because where one is omitted by a study it is sometimes possible to use the others, thus serving the purpose of secondary analysis. No one will be fully satisfied with our choices, but that is the nature of preliminary research in a new and untested topic.

Most of these variables are, in fact, general categories. For example, occupation may refer to respondent's occupation, or to that of several other people. *One of the recommendations we feel impelled to make is that the referents of a variable be made clear in a study's documentation, preferably through the inclusion in code books of the exact question asked.* Although we shall deal with this in connection with specific variables, a general warning is in order: scholars doing secondary analysis must exercise caution in comparing categories in different surveys, because even when the coded categories are identical. the question may not be equivalent. For example, 'income' may refer to last year's, this year's, or some average; it may refer to an individual's or a family's income. And so on, with many other variables.

List of Variables

1) age (or date of birth)
2) sex
3) race
4) marital status
5) own or rent home
6) organizational membership (number, type and degree of activity)
7) size of community of residence (now, as child, etc.)
8) length of residence in community
9) number of intra-Canada moves

10)location of intra-Canada moves (inter-provincial)

11)size of family or of household, number of children, etc.

12)relationship to head of household

13)occupation (current, former, respondent's, head of household's, R's father or mother's, R,s spouse, etc.)

14)income (respondent's, head of household's, family's, etc.)

15)education (formal schooling, vocational, apprenticeship, etc.)

16)social class (respondent's self-perception, interviewer's assessment)

17)religious affiliation

18)language (mother tongue, language spoken in home, language of interview, etc.)

19)nativity (country of birth, parents' birthplace)

20)ethnicity (ethnic origin, ethnic identification, etc.)

21)activity in political parties

22)party identification

23)voting record

V Frequency of Occurrence of Variables

Of the variables examined here, some are to be found in most surveys while many are rare. Some surveys contain questions related to almost all the variables while others contain only a limited set. In the following pages we shall attempt to describe the relative frequency of the different variables under consideration and to relate their occurrence to various explanatory factors.

The tables presented show overall results for all studies examined followed by results for 'English' and 'French' language studies separately.[8] 'French' tables are divided, where relevant, into those in which the fieldwork was done or the instrument prepared by the Centre de Sondage (Centre for Survey Research, University of Montreal) and those done by other agencies or individuals. The reason for this latter division is that the relative degree of standardization achieved by that organization may, in some cases, be wholly or partly responsible for apparent trends in 'French' studies.

Tables 1 to 4 present summaries of the number of variables included according to the topic of the study, the sampling base, the year, and the method of data collection. These tables also give an indication of the extent to which the surveys considered for this study cover a range of topics, time periods, locales and data gathering techniques. It is impossible to state whether these distributions differ significantly from the total universe of Canadian social surveys.

Certain clear trends do, however, appear to emerge from the tables. When 'topic' is considered (Table 1), studies falling into the broad categories of election and opinion polls, and acculturation and socialization studies tend to comprise more socio-demographic variables than do surveys of students and career groups. The percentage of studies including at least 10 such variables among the former category ranges from 58% to 68%, while among the latter it is only 29%. Similarly Table 2 would indicate that geographically based samples produce greater numbers of variables than do institutionally based ones (56%-74%, as against 33%, have 10 or more variables). According to the results we have obtained it would appear also that the larger the geographic scope of the study the greater the number of variables.

'Topic' as defined here and 'sample base' are to a large extent overlapping distinctions and thus similar explana-

Table 1
Distribution of Variables by Topic of Survey*
(without distinction by language)

	Type of Survey						
Number of Variables**	Election Study	Public Opinion Poll	Student and Career-Groups	Employ-ment	Accultur-ation and Socializ-ation	Other	Total
2-9	8 (38)	11 (42)	15 (71)	6	11 (32)	8	59 (42)
10-14	6 (29)	12 (46)	6 (29)	4	19 (56)	5	52 (41)
15 or more	7 (33)	3 (12)	0 (0)	0	4 (12)	1	15 (12)
Total	21(100)	26(100)	21(100)	10	34(100)	14(100)	126(100)

*Vertical percentages shown in parentheses where appropriate.

**No study asked less than two of the 23 variables; the largest number asked was 22 out of 23.

Distribution of Variables by Topic of Survey and Language

	English-language Surveys						
Number of Variables	Election Study	Public Opinion Poll	Student and Career-Groups	Employ-ment	Accultur-ation and Socializ-ation	Other	Total
2-9	0	1	6	5	2	2	16
10-14	3	6	4	1	1	2	17
15 or more	7	2	0	0	2	1	12
Total	10	9	10	6	5	5	45
	French-language Surveys						
2-9	8	10	9	1	9	6	43
10-14	3	6	2	3	18	3	35
15 or more	0	1	0	0	2	0	3
Total	11	17	11	4	29	9	81

Table 2
Distribution of Variables by Sample Base*
(without distinction by language)

Number of Variables	National	Provincial	Sub-provincial	Institution	Other	Total
2–9	5 (26)	12 (41)	15 (44)	24 (67)	3	59 (47)
10–14	10 (53)	13 (45)	13 (38)	11 (30)	5	52 (41)
15 or more	4 (21)	4 (14)	6 (18)	1 (3)	0	15 (12)
Total	19(100)	29(100)	34(100)	36(100)	8	126(100)

*Vertical percentages shown in parentheses where appropriate.

Distribution of Variables by Sample Base and Language

English-language Surveys

Number of Variables	National	Provincial	Sub-provincial	Institution	Other	Total
2–9	3	3	5	3	2	16
10–14	6	4	4	1	2	17
15 or more	4	3	5	0	0	12
Total	13	10	14	4	4	45

French-language Surveys

Number of Variables	National	Provincial	Sub-provincial	Institution	Other	Total
2–9	2	9	10	21	1	43
10–14	4	9	9	10	3	35
15 or more	0	1	1	1	0	3
Total	6	19	20	32	4	81

tions may be used to account for the differences noted above. As observed earlier, a number of variables considered in the present report relate primarily to a household. It is therefore to be expected that they will occur more frequently in household-based surveys than in institutionally based research where the object of interest is the individual in a non-household context. Thus the intrinsic usefulness of some variables is diminished in studies of specialized groups or institutional populations, and to this extent their absence is no cause for concern. However, the circumstances in which such studies are often conducted also contribute to the smaller numbers of variables they contain. There is a tendency for institutional studies to be carried out by an investigator without adequate funding and therefore to be kept brief or highly focused. Frequently also they are conducted by members of the organization or groups under study, without specialized professional help — officers of professional associations distribute questionnaires among their own members, students conduct surveys of other students. Understandably such persons are often too involved in the short-term goal envisaged to appreciate the possibilities their data could offer for secondary analysis. The poor quality and limited scope of many such studies provide arguments for further education in the re-use potential of survey data.

Table 3 suggests that no clear trend over time exists toward including either more or fewer variables, the differences observed in the overall figures being too slight to be significant. The fact that among the English-language studies the earlier period has a higher proportion of variables reflects mainly the inclusion of several geographically based election studies in those years, while the apparent increase in the number of variables included in the French-language studies after 1970 is entirely due to the fact that all but one of the Centre de Sondage studies examined belong to that period.

The link between the number of variables included and the method of data collection emerges quite clearly from Table 4. This may indeed be the single most important factor in determining the number of variables measured.[9] The highest number of variables is to be found in studies using personal interviews. The time constraint is of course less acute in a personal interview and, once an interview has been agreed to, an efficient interviewer working with a well-designed schedule should have no trouble eliciting a

Table 3
Distribution of Variables by Date of Survey*
(without distinction by language)

Number of Variables	1960-1969	1970-1974	Date Not Known	Total
2-9	19 (43)	35 (47)	5	59 (47)
10-14	17 (39)	33 (44)	2	52 (41)
15 or more	8 (18)	7 (9)	0	15 (12)
Total	44 (100)	75 (100)	7	126 (100)

*Vertical percentages shown in parentheses.

Distribution of Variables by Date of Survey and Language

English-language Surveys

Number of Variables	1960-1969	1970-1974	Date Not Known	Total
2-9	5	8	3	16
10-14	9	6	2	17
15 or more	8	4	0	12
Total	22	18	5	45

French-language Surveys

Number of Variables		1960-1969	1970-1974	Date Not Known	Total
2-9	CS*	1	19	0	20
	Others	13	8	2	23
	Total	14	27	2	43
10-14	CS	0	25	0	25
	Others	8	2	0	10
	Total	8	27	0	35
15 or more	CS	0	3	0	3
	Others	0	0	0	0
	Total	0	3	0	3
Total	CS	1	47	0	48
	Others	21	10	2	33
	Total	22	57	2	81

*CS means Centre de Sondage studies.

Table 4
Distribution of Variables by Data Collection Method
(without distinction by language)

Number of Variables	Personal Interview	Telephone Interview	Self-administered	Unknown	Total
2–9	24	9	22	3	58
10–14	34	2	14	3	53
15 or more	13	0	1	1	15
Total	71	11	37	7	126

Distribution of Variables by Data Collection Method and Language

English-language Surveys

Number of Variables	Personal Interview	Telephone Interview	Self-administered	Unknown	Total
2–9	4	0	9	3	16
10–14	9	0	5	3	17
15 or more	10	0	1	1	12
Total	23	0	15	7	45

French-language Surveys

Number of Variables	Personal Interview	Telephone Interview	Self-administered	Total
2-9	20	9	13	42
10-14	25	2	9	36
15 or more	3	0	0	3
Total	48	11	22	81

satisfactory amount of background information long before the limits of respondent tolerance are reached.

Rapport, moreover, may more easily be established in a face-to-face situation; also devices such as flash cards may be used where appropriate, and probing techniques may more readily be applied, all of which facilitate the task of obtaining personal information. For similar reasons the potential for detailed responses is also increased, providing richer material for coding. Last but not least, though of course the per-unit cost of interviews is high, the initial investment required for training, travel and call-backs is affected little by the addition of a handful of basic socio-demographic items. Five to ten minutes should be quite adequate to cover these for most practical purposes, and this represents a minimal extra investment in the context of the average 45 to 60 minute interview. There is therefore little excuse for personal interview studies failing to elicit sufficient information for purposes of secondary analysis. Fortunately the studies we examined show general, if not universal, recognition of this fact; and though the material is by no means always comparable from one study to another, the quantity at least is usually within acceptable limits.

Telephone interviews clearly do not, and cannot, elicit the same quantity or richness of material. The normal maximum duration of a telephone interview is about a third of the average duration of a personal interview. Rapport is more difficult to achieve, personal information is more reluctantly provided, and mid-interview refusals are always a hazard if items are perceived as threatening.

These considerations are not intended, however, to increase the traditional academic mistrust of telephone surveys. On the contrary there is much to be said for telephone interviewing. Such surveys may be conducted with great speed, and their cost is a mere fraction of that of personal interviews; besides, techniques such as random digit dialing have substantially improved the reliability of telephone samples, and increased use of the telephone may be one solution to the problem of declining response rates encountered with traditional interviewing methods. *In short, for many purposes telephone surveys are a viable alternative, and within the context of the present report they may well be fertile terrain for the introduction of standardized variables.* Indeed, when constructing more elaborate research instruments researchers often have legitimate reasons for using extensive and innovative forms of socio-demographic variables which do not lend themselves to comparative analysis. The typical telephone survey instrument, on the other hand, contains a basic set of concise background questions with simplified responses, and these afford somewhat better possibilities for standardization. Moreover, while it is true that, on an individual study basis, telephone surveys provide less material for secondary analysis, they could, if a minimum of standardization is reached, constitute a valuable source of material for comparative analysis across time periods and locales, thus achieving a most impressive cost-benefit ratio.

Self-administered questionnaires, it will be noted, appear to include somewhat more socio-demographic variables than telephone surveys. They are, of course, beset by some of the same time constraints as telephone surveys. In addition, when conducted by mail they suffer from acute response rate problems which often render them somewhat unreliable for primary analysis and even more so for secondary or comparative analysis. For this reason our recommendations will be directed more to the possibilities of standardizing personal interview and telephone survey instruments; the special needs of mailed questionnaires deserve separate and detailed investigation.

Table 5 gives an idea of the overall frequency of the variables in relation to one another. Some explanation must be offered for the precise meaning of the table and the significance of the figures it contains.

First of all, when it is indicated that a variable is 'measured more than one way' this does not necessarily mean that the same question was asked several times or the same information elicited. As already mentioned, what we refer to as 'variables' are in fact groups of related aspects of given characteristics. Thus when a variable is said to have been measured 'more than once' this means that more than one aspect of the characteristic, relating to different time-periods or different persons, have been measured. A few examples will clarify this distinction. At least one aspect of 'occupation' was measured in 39 English-language surveys, and in 30 of these some additional aspect was also covered. These latter included respondent's second occupation, spouse's occupation, occupation of respondent's father, occupation of other wage-earners in family, and several other more rare questions such as respondent's mother's occupation.

Income can obviously refer to similar categories. Education was ascertained in some cases not only for the respondent but also for the respondent's father or spouse. Age was sometimes estimated by interviewer as well as directly asked.

Ethnicity and nativity were asked more than once because a distinction was sometimes made between the background of the respondent's father (ancestral origins or birthplace, where raised as a child) and the respondent's mother.

Social class was sometimes measured by interviewer assessment in addition to direct questioning of respondent or questioning about respondent's father.

Size of family depends on the total number of persons in the household, but in several cases questions were also asked about the number of school age or preschool children or by age category. (See the later discussion of this variable for some problems of definition of 'family' and 'household'.)

Party identification, party activity, and voting record reveal multiple questioning mainly because separate questions were often asked about federal and provincial levels.

It is important when reading Table 5 to keep in mind the all-inclusiveness of the variable categories used in order that the nature of the findings may be fully appreciated. A category such as 'occupation' or 'language' comprises a number of very different items of information all of which may or may not be relevant to the needs of a given study in terms of secondary analysis, and the fact that a study did in fact measure some aspect of a variable does not automatically mean that the most appropriate form of the variable was included. For example, in a number of studies which can be said to have measured 'language,' the actual information elicited was 'language of interview' instead of some more reliable indicator of linguistic affiliation. Similarly, studies occasionally confine themselves to ascertaining respondent's occupational status (employed, unemployed, retired, etc.) omitting occupation as such, thus providing virtually no usable information for purposes of

Table 5A
Frequency of Occurrence of Each Variable*
(without distinction by Language)

Variable	No. of surveys in which variable is:			
	not measured	measured	total	measured more than one way
1. Age	12 (10)	114 (90)	126(100)	21 (17)
2. Sex	19 (15)	107 (85)	126(100)	2 (2)
3. Race	122 (97)	4 (3)	126(100)	0 (0)
4. Marital Status	39 (31)	87 (69)	126(100)	2 (2)
5. Size of Household	58 (46)	68 (54)	126(100)	21 (17)
6. Relationship to Head of Household	86 (68)	40 (32)	126(100)	0 (0)
7. Own or Rent Home	95 (75)	31 (25)	126(100)	3 (2)
8. Size of Place of Residence	69 (55)	57 (45)	126(100)	15 (12)
9. Length of Residence in Community	86 (68)	40 (32)	126(100)	5 (4)
10. No. of Intra-Canada Moves	114 (90)	12 (10)	126(100)	2 (2)
11. Location of Intra-Canada Moves	112 (89)	14 (11)	126(100)	3 (2)
12. Social Class	101 (80)	25 (20)	126(100)	5 (4)
13. Occupation	11 (9)	115 (91)	126(100)	79 (63)
14. Income	38 (30)	88 (70)	126(100)	28 (22)
15. Education	9 (7)	117 (93)	126(100)	58 (46)
16. Religion	64 (51)	62 (49)	126(100)	31 (25)
17. Language	53 (42)	73 (58)	126(100)	39 (31)
18. Ethnicity	72 (57)	54 (43)	126(100)	14 (11)
19. Nativity	69 (55)	57 (45)	126(100)	26 (21)
20. Organizational Membership	74 (59)	59 (41)	126(100)	29 (23)
21. Activity in Political Parties	105 (83)	21 (17)	126(100)	18 (14)
22. Party Identification	94 (75)	32 (25)	126(100)	25 (20)
23. Voting Record	92 (73)	34 (27)	126(100)	28 (22)

* horizontal percentages shown in parentheses.

Table 5B
Frequency of Occurrence of each Variable
(English)

Variable	No. of surveys in which variable is:		
	not measured	measured	measured more than one way
1. Age	6	39	8
2. Sex	5	40	0
3. Race	43	2	0
4. Marital Status	16	29	0
5. Size of Household	25	20	9
6. Relationship to Head of Household	31	14	0
7. Own or Rent Home	30	15	0
8. Size of Place of Residence	37	8	0
9. Length of Residence in Community	27	18	0
10. No. of Intra-Canada Moves	38	7	2
11. Location of Intra-Canada Moves	38	7	1
12. Social Class	26	19	4
13. Occupation	6	39	30
14. Income	12	33	10
15. Education	2	43	19
16. Religion	12	33	12
17. Language	21	24	10
18. Ethnicity	21	24	7
19. Nativity	17	28	15
20. Organizational Membership	23	22	7
21. Activity in Political Parties	35	10	8
22. Party Identification	25	20	17
23. Voting Record	28	17	15

Table 5C
Frequency of Occurrence of Each Variable
(French)

Variable	No. of surveys in which variable is:								
	not measured			measured			measured more than one way		
	CS*	Others	Total	CS*	Others	Total	CS*	Others	Total
1. Age	4	2	6	44	31	75	10	3	13
2. Sex	6	8	14	42	25	67	2	0	2
3. Race	47	32	79	1	1	2	0	0	0
4. Marital Status	15	8	23	33	25	58	2	0	2
5. Size of Household	15	18	33	33	15	48	7	5	12
6. Relationship to Head of Household	25	30	55	23	3	26	0	0	0
7. Own or Rent Home	35	30	65	13	3	16	3	0	3
8. Size of Place of Residence	12	20	32	36	13	49	15	0	15
9. Length of Residence in Community	34	25	59	14	8	22	4	1	5
10. No. of Intra-Canada Moves	43	33	76	5	0	5	0	0	0
11. Location of Intra-Canada Moves	43	31	74	5	2	7	1	1	2
12. Social Class	43	32	75	5	1	6	1	0	1
13. Occupation	0	5	5	48	28	76	40	9	49
14. Income	17	9	26	31	24	55	14	4	18
15. Education	2	5	7	46	28	74	30	9	39
16. Religion	26	26	52	22	7	29	15	4	19
17. Language	11	21	32	37	12	49	25	4	29
18. Ethnicity	32	19	51	16	14	30	7	0	7
19. Nativity	31	21	52	17	12	29	6	5	11
20. Organizational Membership	31	20	51	17	13	30	11	11	22
21. Activity in Political Parties	42	28	70	6	5	11	5	5	10
22. Party Identification	42	27	69	6	6	12	3	5	8
23. Voting Record	39	25	64	9	8	17	7	6	13

*CS means Centre de Sondage studies

defining social status. Hence some of the figures in Table 5 may give an over-optimistic picture of the frequency of some variables.

On the other hand these distinctions may partly be offset when one considers that certain variables are quite legitimately omitted from certain types of studies, either because the information they provide is implicitly contained in the eligibility criteria used for sampling, or because the context makes them quite simply irrelevant. For example, when sampling procedure defines eligible persons as married women, then, provided sampling information is available, there is clearly no point in coding 'sex' and 'marital status.' Likewise, if a study is conducted in a community known to be 95% francophone it may well be unnecessary to ask about 'language.'

Ideally a judgment would have to be made about the relevance of each variable within the context of each study. However, such an investigation would require detailed analysis of the many possible functions of individual variables for both primary and secondary analysis, and this is beyond the scope of this report.

What is clear from Table 5 is that some variables are almost universally present while others are rarely included. Race and variables concerned with geographic mobility are among the latter. The most frequently encountered variables, as might be anticipated, are those related to basic personal characteristics (sex, age, marital status) and those commonly used to measure social status or 'class' (particularly education and occupation). Ethnically related variables are somewhat less common, as are those connected with place of residence and household related variables. It is reasonable to postulate that some of these variations in frequency are inevitable since they are connected with the relevance of each type of variable to different types of topics and populations, the commoner variables being relevant to virtually all contexts, while less frequent variables apply only to given research contexts. For instance, household related variables (size of family, respondent relationship to head) are clearly of importance mainly in studies using household based samples, while ethnic related variables are most pertinent in ethnically heterogeneous populations. Nevertheless, examples of under-use and over-use of certain variables or aspects of variables are apparent in some cases, and these will be raised individually later in the report.

Another phenomenon which emerges from Table 5 is that while some socio-demographic variables do occur with some regularity as background items (usually as a single simple question), others occur more rarely but when they are present they are usually measured in greater detail. This is notably the case for organizational membership, geographic mobility, and the various forms of political activity. We infer from this pattern that such variables are not generally used by researchers as background material but as research subjects in themselves.

In the remarks made in later sections of this report we will be more concerned with some variables than with others. Those which are very infrequent will generally not be given much attention. Others, such as age and sex, which occur frequently but with relatively little variety in questioning and coding will also be disposed of quickly. Most of the attention in this report will therefore be reserved for variables which are common but which exhibit great variance in question format and coding scheme, and for those which seem to us to be underused for various reasons. Occupation, education, ethnicity, nativity, religion, social class, and the variables concerned with household information and political parties will receive disproportionate amounts of space.

Several variables occasion little difficulty in standardization. There are different reasons for this — agreement on measurement, easily corrected inadequacies, or infrequency of use.

Age

Most of the surveys examined here measured the age of respondents. There was some variety in question format and coding. Some studies asked for date of birth, others asked age in years or age in terms of a range of years (under 25, 25-34, etc.). About half of the surveys used some form of pre-coded response, such as 5- or 10-year categories, and a few used a flash card with pre-coded answers.

Coding schemes also reveal considerable variety. Among English studies about three-quarters code age, whereas only a quarter code year of birth; French studies divide about half and half. Some of each type (age or date) are coded directly, while some are collapsed into categories. Unfortunately, there are nearly as many ways of coding in categories as there are studies (more than 30 different schemes) and the widely differing limits of the categories used render them almost universally incompatible with one another. In some cases there are only three or four categories, although most have more than seven.

Clearly, then, this variable does afford some re-use potential, since coding age in years, exact date of birth, or a large number of categories allows other scholars flexibility in secondary analysis. *It seems reasonable, however, to urge strongly that all future surveys code exact year of birth or exact age in years for maximum flexibility.* (Incidentally, either of these procedures results in a ratio scale.) An investigator (principal or secondary) can easily score these into categories or cohorts. Normally date of birth will be found to be preferable when a respondent is asked about his own age, this being more readily recalled and less liable to be a source of embarrassment than actual age. On the other hand, when information is asked about other people 'age in years' will be the easier approach. Occasionally, when a researcher has good reason to assume that exact age will not be known, pre-coded categories may be justified to avoid non-response (e.g., when asking children about their parents' ages).

Date of birth (for respondent)

'In what year were you born?'
Year:

Coding requires two columns: last two digits of year.

Alternative (when respondent gives age of other persons)
'How old is....?'
Age:
*Coding requires two columns: '99' can include all re-
spondents 100 or more years old.*

Sex

There is no need for concern here, as sex is always coded by
interviewer assessment or a pre-coded category (if self-
administered). Even telephone interviews should pose few
problems.

Race

This is so uncommon it occasions little difficulty. When
asked, the only concern is 1)what 'race' means and 2)how
many categories are used. The two elements are related,
but in ways which go beyond our needs in this report. (We
shall return briefly to this variable when discussing ethnicity below.)

Marital Status

There is a clear norm for closed (pre-coded) questions for
this variable. Furthermore, the questions are similar in
format: no flashcards, no screening questions, and no
probes. Coding, on the other hand, shows some variety,
but not enough to give concern to most scholars. All coding schemes have categories for married and single, but
differ in whether the following categories are separate or
combined in various ways: separated, divorced, widowed,
or common law. About one-third of the schemes have five
categories — all of the above except common law; another
third use only four categories, 'separated' and 'divorced'
being grouped together, doubtless on the grounds that it is
the absence of one or other spouse from the household
which is relevant to most social research objectives rather
than the precise legal status of the relationship. Categories
either allowing for common law marriages as a separate
possibility, or grouping them explicitly with conventional
marriages are on the increase, especially in studies dealing
with student samples or low-income areas. This is proba-

bly a good thing in terms of gaining realistic information about the household's socio-economic status; however the benefits should be weighed in individual cases against the interviewing problems a separate category for 'common law' may create in some social contexts. A variant peculiar to Quebec, but fairly frequent in that province, is the inclusion of 'religious' as a separate category. This, however, is only relevant in limited contexts (e.g., in surveys of Quebec teachers) and for most purposes may be grouped with 'single.'

Marital status
'Are you presently....'[11]
married? (including common law)[12]
widowed?
divorced?
separated?
single? (never married, including religious)

Own or Rent Home

When asked, a closed question or flashcard was almost always used. This question also frequently ascertained if the home (or farm) was owned or under a mortgage, although this was not found among the French studies examined. If the respondent rented the dwelling, he was sometimes asked if he had any plans to purchase a house. These two latter items are useful information but are not essential for most purposes. It is sometimes useful to have categories for 'roomer' or lodger, and 'rent free.'

'Is this dwelling....'
owned or being bought by you (or a member of this household)? rented (even if no cash rent is paid to the landlord)?

VII Variables Which Pose More Complex Problems

Organizational Membership

This variable, when asked, is usually intended to reflect the organizational affiliation of respondent or head of household. In some studies, however, membership is scored for spouse separately. (One qualification to bear in mind: party membership is a permissible response here, in most surveys, but we shall deal below with that form of membership when it is ascertained separately.) Approximately three-quarters of the questions asking about this mentioned predetermined types of organizations, and those that were open-ended specified that the interviewer should probe for precise information on the nature of organizations.

Very little information was lost in coding, but very few surveys touched on the subject at all. In nearly every case, when a pre-coded question was asked, all of the responses were coded. In English-language studies, the median number of types of organization coded was 9; the range was from 2 to 88. The most frequently coded types of organizations overall were: trade unions and professional and trade associations, sports and recreations clubs, ethnic associations, political organizations, and religious groups. Which organizations were combined into what categories presents a bewildering variety of patterns. Also those surveys which do contain information on the subject usually go beyond just ascertaining membership and attempt to measure activity within organizations. The most frequently used questions in this respect concern holding office within the organizations and attendance at meetings.

Membership in organizations

This subject may be approached in two different ways. Either the respondent is asked whether he belongs to any organizations, associations, or groups and is asked to specify which, or specific types of organizations or groups are mentioned to him and he is asked whether he belongs to any of these. In either case the range of organizations covered may vary widely; a list of the most frequently occurring ones in Canada is given below.[13]

'Do you belong to any kind of organizations, associations or groups, such as ....?'

Examples may be chosen from list below.
No
Yes
'Could you tell me their names, and the main activity or
aim of each one?'

Alternative
'Do you belong to ....?'
Mention type of organization.
Code 'yes' or 'no' for each organization in following list.

Types of organizations most frequently encountered
professional associations
trade associations
chambers of commerce
labour unions
tenants' associations
landlords' associations
citizens' organizations
educational organizations
religious organizations
charitable organizations
youth organizations
ethnic associations
fraternal and voluntary organizations
political organizations
cooperative organizations
sports associations
other leisure associations
social clubs and organizations

Extent of activity within organizations
'Do you attend meetings or take part in activities orga-
nized by (organization) or do voluntary work for it?'
No
Yes
'In an average month, how many hours would you say you
spend at meetings or activities organized by (organi-
zation) or doing voluntary work for it?'
Number of hours per month:

'Thinking about meetings or other activities organized by (organization), would you say you attend:'

all of them (or almost all)?

most of them?

some of them?

none (attended)?

none are held.

'Do you hold any kind of office with the organization (such as secretary or treasurer) or do you serve on any committee?'

Yes

No

'Apart from any compulsory membership fee, do you make any voluntary financial contribution to the (organization)?'

Yes

No

Size of Place of Residence

This variable refers to the size or type of community in which the respondent currently lives (or formerly lived). Although not included often in English-language surveys examined, it was more frequent in French-language studies. Information on the subject is derived from various sources. In many cases what is actually coded is geographical location rather than the size or type of place of residence, as for example when the name of each city or locality included in the sample is given a unique code. When this happens the problem of exact boundaries arises; what does it mean, for example, when a respondent is said to live in 'Toronto,' or in 'Montreal-south'? Obviously very different types of habitat may be included under these headings, particularly when the category is chosen on the basis of an educated (or uneducated) guess on the part of respondent, interviewer, or coder rather than on precise cartography. Many studies using area based samples also code geographical location as part of the respondent's identification number; this may take the form of an enumeration area, census tract, or electoral riding number. While precise, this can pose two kinds of problems. The significance of the digits of the ID number is often not documented in the code book, and, when documented the actual area numbers may not be classified according to ecological criteria either, leaving secondary users with the bothersome task of looking up the precise location of each primary sampling unit. When information is obtained explicitly in terms of *size* of place of residence by means of a question, pre-coded categories are the rule but there is some variety in the category boundaries. Many do not distinguish farm from non-farm, some fail to differentiate suburb from city core, and in between these extremes the number of categories varies from two to seven. *Of course, in some cases size of community is not a variable (for example, in a study of one city area), but it would be useful if even then the principal investigator indicated in the code book the size of the community in which the study was conducted.*

For those questions asking about the size of the community in which the respondent grew up, rather than current residence, the respondent must generally be asked to estimate it.[14] *Otherwise we recommend it be ascertained by coders or interviewers from official data and coded into the suggested categories below* (or more, if an investigator needs additional detail).

Size of present place of residence from address or sampling information[15]

Whenever possible, size of present place of residence should be coded from respondent's address using official data to determine the correct category. This may be done by coders after the survey has taken place, or, alternatively, sampling technicians may pre-code the information. In either case codes are as follows:

rural — farm
rural — non-farm
1,000 — 2,499 inhabitants
2,500 — 4,999
5,000 — 9,999
10,000 — 29,999
30,000 — 59,999
60,000 — 99,999

100,000 – 499,999[16]
500,000 and more[16]

Alternative

Size of present place of residence from question to respondent[17]

When address of respondent is not known (e.g., in an anonymous mail-out survey, telephone survey, or when respondent is contacted at school or work) a direct question may be necessary:

'In what kind of a place do you live at present?'
on a farm
in the open country, but not on a farm
in a small village (1,000-2,499 inhabitants)
in a large village (2,500-4,999 inhabitants)
in a small town (5,000-9,999 inhabitants)
in a town of 10,000-29,999 inhabitants
in a city of 30,000-59,999 inhabitants
in a city of 60,000-99,999 inhabitants
in a city of 100,000-499,999 inhabitants
in a city of over 500,000 inhabitants

Greater accuracy will be achieved by asking respondent to name his place of residence, and coding size later from above code:

'In what city, town, village or rural area do you live at present?'
Name:
If in a rural area
'Do you live....'
on a farm?
in open country, but not on a farm?

Size of former place(s) of residence

For maximum precision actual place may be asked and size coded from official data for the appropriate period of time. Usually, however, an estimate from the respondent must suffice, for example:

Size of place of residence during childhood

'In what kind of a place did you spend most of your time when you were a child, that is, up to age 16?'[18]
Code according to above categories.

We strongly recommend more systematic inclusion of residential variables in geographic based samples, as it constitutes a basic minimum of information for purposes of ecological analysis.

Length of Residence in Community

Half the time, when asked, this variable was measured by an open-ended question, and half by a pre-coded one. Apparently, no probes or flashcards were used in any study. As with so many variables, very little information was coded. For example, despite open-ended questions which might be answered by phrases like 'less than 3 months,' '26 years,' or whatever, many studies have coded responses into crude categories like 'less than 5 years,' '5-20 years,' 'all the time.'

We recommend that finer categories be used, particularly when coding responses that indicate short duration in a locale. Since this variable will generally be taken as an indicator of 'integration' into the community, the differences among two months, a year, and five years is very great. Coding the exact number of years (with a separate category for periods of less than a year) should prove no more difficult than for age, where exact coding is quite common.

For the actual question used, 'community' is a somewhat ambiguous word, as well as not having exact French-English equivalents, and *it would be well to substitute 'city,' 'town,' 'village,' or locality, as appropriate,* when this is what is intended. Alternatively 'neighbourhood' may be psychologically more real in many cases, and a number of studies use this word specifically. Several French-language studies narrowed the question still further by asking about length of time at present address. (Statistics Canada frequently asks 'how long have you lived in this dwelling?' This is too specific for most purposes.) The choice between the various possible questions must be made according to the theoretical focus of the study.

Length of residence
'How long have you been living in this city (town, village, etc.)?'

Number of years:

Less than one year

Alternative

Date of arrival in present place of residence
'When did you first come to live in this city (town, village, etc.)?'
Month:
Year:
In both cases, use actual numeric codes.

Number of Intra-Canada Moves

Although a simple variable in principle, the base year problem makes coded responses unreliable for cross-analysis. For example, different surveys ask for the number of times respondent has moved: in lifetime, since June 1, 1958, in last five years, or since age 16. Responses clearly vary with the base year used. One good sign, however, is that coding is usually in terms of the exact number of moves, one, two, and so on, up to 10 or more.

Although not asked often, and virtually absent as a direct question from the French-language studies examined, this question has some potential for sociological analysis. *We therefore feel compelled to recommend that, where feasible, investigators ask about the number of moves in lifetime.* If additional information is required, a second question can probe for more recent moves (since a given age or date). It would also be advantageous to clarify whether the question refers to all kinds of moves or only to intercity moves.

'How many times have you moved from one Canadian city, town, village, or municipality to another (during your lifetime) (in the past five years, etc.)?'[19]
Moving away and returning to the same place should be counted as two moves.

Number of moves:
Code actual number of moves.

Location of Intra-Canada Moves

This variable has generally been asked in terms of a list of the provinces in which respondent has lived. Sometimes respondents are asked also to list provinces in which they have visited. There is some variety in coding schemes, but *the norm is obvious: a code for each province.*

A peculiarity we noted concerns the fact that only in studies particularly concerned with mobility do the questionnaires ascertain whether these moves involved changes from urban to rural or rural to urban situations. This obvious gap is easily remedied by including a supplementary question whenever mobility is of interest. Such a question could be coded according to the categories recommended for size of place. Similar information is, however, to be found in those studies which coded both size of current place of residence and size of place of birth or of residence during childhood.

'In which other Canadian provinces have you lived for more than 6 months?'[20]
Check all applicable.
Newfoundland
Prince Edward Island
Nova Scotia
New Brunswick
Quebec
Ontario
Manitoba
Saskatchewan
Alberta
British Columbia
Yukon
Northwest Territories

A less informative but perhaps quicker alternative formulation would be:
'Have you ever lived (for more than six months) in any other Canadian province besides this one?'
(*If yes*) 'How many?'
No
Yes
Number:

Mobility variables in general are either passed over completely by researchers or examined in great detail; for example, a number of studies asked respondents to list the various addresses at which they have resided, together with the dates they moved in and moved out. The key aspects of mobility singled out above ('length of residence,' 'number of moves,' etc.) can clearly be derived from this. Particularly in the French-language studies we looked at, either very detailed information was elicited or none at all. Possibly the development of a sub-set of easily coded questions to cover important dimensions of residential mobility would enhance the coverage of this topic when it is not the prime focus of the study.

Household Information

1.Size of Household or Family

There is considerable confusion in the literature and among survey organizations about the distinctions among households, families, and other residential units. We are not prepared to legislate on this matter, but it may be helpful to quote the Statistics Canada definition of 'household' (in contrast to a 'family' composed of biologically or legally related individuals):

'A household is any person or group of persons occupying a dwelling. It may consist of a family group with or without servants, lodgers, etc., or a group of unrelated persons sharing a dwelling, one person living alone, staff members, employees or permanent residents of hotels, motels, institutions, if they have no usual place of residence elsewhere.'[21]

To a large extent, the choice of sampling frame resolves this confusion for a given survey. *We recommend, however, that investigators indicate the definitions used, in the code book or other documentation. This is especially vital if they deviate from Statistics Canada practice.* Below, in discussing income, the distinction between household and family becomes particularly important.

Despite its obvious use in relation to socio-economic variables, particularly income, less than half the household-based surveys we examined obtained information on size of household or size of family. Even when this information is obtained, its usefulness is diminished by the fact that often the basic question is qualified in terms of age (for example, the number in the household above age 12, or age 15, or age 18, etc.). Often the reason for this is that

the source of the coded information is the list of household
members drawn up prior to random selection of the respondent, and the interviewer is given instructions to list
only those eligible for interview, that is, those over a certain age. In some cases also the number of persons in several different age groups is asked, and here coding varies
according to whether the original distinctions by age are
preserved or collapsed. Generally, quite a bit of collapsing
is common in such cases. When the variable takes the
form 'number of children,' again the age limits vary considerably, and actual numbers are frequently grouped in
coding, with very little justification since possible number
of categories is seldom very large.

Size and composition of household from list of household
members[22]

Interviewer obtains list of household members for purposes of selecting respondent. Usually order of list is: head,
spouse (if any), other relatives by order of age, non-relatives by order of age. Relationship to head, sex, age, and
marital status are noted for each, as well as other characteristics (e.g., mother tongue) if required for selection purposes. If possible, all the above information is coded for
each person using coding conventions for individual variables (age, sex, etc.) and the following detailed relationship
code:

head

spouse of head

son or daughter of head

father or mother of head

brother or sister of head

son-in-law or daughter-in-law of head

father-in-law or mother-in-law of head

brother-in-law or sister-in-law of head

grandson or granddaughter of head

nephew or niece of head

other relative of head (*specify*)

lodger

spouse of lodger

child of lodger

other non-relative (*specify*)

Alternative coding scheme

Using the same household list, minimum information may be coded at lesser cost as follows:

Head of household: male/female (1 col), age (2 col)

Spouse: age (2 col)

Children of head: number (2 col)

Other relatives: number (2 col)

Non-relatives: number (2 col)

Total number of persons: number (2 col)
Alternative is quicker, but gains less information.

Size of household from direct question
'How many persons, *including yourself,* usually live in this household? Please count all persons who normally live here, whether they are relatives or not.'

Number of persons:

In addition to information on the basic composition of the household (family), some investigators may wish to ask some of the following supplementary questions.

Number of children
'How many children do you have?'[23]
Number:

Number of children in household
'How many of your children live here with you?'
Number:

Number of economically dependent children
'How many of your children are dependent on you for financial support?'
Number:

Number of dependents
'How many persons living in this household are dependent on you (head) for financial support?'
Number:

Number of persons contributing to household income
'How many persons in this household receive income from work, such as salaries, wages, commissions, or tips?'
Number:

'How many persons in this household receive income from other sources, such as pensions, family allowances, investments, or welfare?'

Number:

In all of these supplementary questions, coding consists of the actual number; therefore, two columns should be allowed for each answer.

2.Relation of Respondent to Head of Household

This variable too is not so frequent as might be expected or desired; again it is present in less than half of the household-based studies. When present, the most common form is: respondent is head of household, or is not head.

Ideally a complete list of household members should have been obtained from the previous question, and their relation to the head of the household (or to each other) should be clear to the interviewer and be coded. For example, besides common categories such as spouse, son, daughter, one might have 'lodger's brother,' 'roommate,' 'son's friend,' etc. This list, which also often comprises sex, age, and marital status of all household members, is the occasion of one of the most frequent losses of information in coding we have observed. Complete coding of it would of course require considerable space on data cards.[24] For purposes of assessing the ability of respondent to answer certain types of questions (e.g., income), it is essential to know who actually answered the questions.

Information may be derived from the household list above or from a direct question as shown below. The same basic code may be used in either case.

Question, if needed
'Are you the head of this household?'
(*If no*) 'What relation, if any, are you to the head of the household?'

Full code

head

spouse of head

son or daughter of head
father or mother of head
brother or sister of head
son-in-law or daughter-in-law of head
father-in-law or mother-in-law of head
brother-in-law or sister-in-law of head
grandson or granddaughter of head
nephew or niece of head
other relative of head (*specify*)
lodger
spouse of lodger
child of lodger
other non-relative of head (*specify*)

Alternative summary code
head
spouse of head
child of head
other relative of head (*specify*)
non-relative (*specify*)

The concept of 'head of household' is of course increasingly being called into question, but it is still in wide use in Canada and no satisfactory substitute appears yet to have been found. We do not feel this report is the place to debate innovations in this respect, but it may prove advisable to include a category such as 'no unique head of household.'

VIII Variables Related to Status

Occupation, income, education, and self-identified (or interviewer assessed) social class constitute different but related facets of social status. Particular citizens will disagree about which aspect most accurately reflects their status; and investigators will place greater emphasis on one or another feature depending on their theoretical or pragmatic orientation. It is, nevertheless, clear that to some degree these four variables are related, and may be assessed jointly for our purposes. Furthermore, as we shall demonstrate, the absence of one or more of these variables from a given survey — which renders it less useful to scholars contemplating secondary analysis — is almost invariably a sign that one of the remaining members of the set will be present. In other words, one or more members of the *cluster* variable called 'status' is available in almost every survey. Thus, part of the ability to do adequate secondary analysis may rest on reconceptualizing one's needs to see how one variable might be substituted for another.

We do not intend by the analysis of these variables as a cluster to imply that there are no problems — or only minor problems — involved in substituting one variable for another. We simply recommend that this be done whenever feasible. Some obstacles to substitutability may be mentioned. First, frequently each of these variables will be related differently to a dependent variable than will possible substitutes. Second, the degree of category detail may make a substitute variable inappropriate. Third, different theories of social stratification require certain indicators but preclude others. Fourth, use of education *as a measure of status* probably requires a simultaneous control for age, given the dramatic increases in education levels in each generation. Thus comparative analysis of studies using different variables from the cluster is not often possible, but further analysis of individual data sets, as well as experimental work constructing indices and hypotheses, may still be feasible.[25]

Our perspective on secondary analysis, moreover, is based on the assumption that it often involves using 'second best.' Second best may refer, as here, to presence or absence of a variable; it may equally refer to coding details, type of sample, geographic extent of sample, or number of cases. Such analysis still has great value, if for no other reason than that it may be a useful pretest for a more focused study. In a world of limited money and potential saturation of certain types of respondents, second best may be the best we can do in many circumstances.

Occupation

This is probably the most difficult variable in any survey as far as both coding and questionnaire design are concerned. This difficulty derives from several related considerations. First, how can one ensure that respondents will provide and interviewers will write down sufficiently detailed information? Job title by itself is unsatisfactory, since it is often ambiguous: for example, 'engineers' build bridges, drive trains, and inspect buildings (as well as occasionally clean toilets). Probes should probably be used. But which? Second, even when one has a detailed job description, often, for reasons of cost, all the information cannot be coded in detail. How many categories should be used? What distinctions are most significant? Third, given a set of categories, complex judgments must be made about their boundaries. This is especially bothersome for occupational codes which are either new or changing their character rapidly. For example, consider the person who repairs technical malfunctions in a computer. Should he be classified with a person who repairs lamps or television sets? Should he be classified as a 'professional' since he will almost surely have a college degree and specialized training? Fourth, to arrive at an accurate description of occupation one frequently must go beyond description of 'activity at work' as such. Sector of employment, self-employed status versus that of employee, part-time or full-time work: all these are valid and often-used distinctions, not to mention the most fundamental one of all — employment status — which distinguishes employed persons from those who have no occupation for a variety of reasons (housewives, retired and unemployed persons, students, etc.). How can one ensure that all relevant items of information are obtained given the many different occupational situations that exist? Finally, whose occupations should be asked about, in what degree of detail, and for what period? Respondent's, head of household's, spouse's or father's occupation? Present, former, or first-ever occupation? Main occupation only or sidelines?

Given such quandaries, it comes as no surprise that surveys vary in the information they elicit and in how they code it. Short of a general theory about the specific aspects of occupational culture which influence (or are influenced by) other social phenomena, one cannot imagine scholars achieving uniformity on this variable. Therefore, for the purposes of secondary analysis, we look for criteria by which to judge the relative adequacy of surveys in this regard. Several are outlined below, the most important of which is the total number of coding categories (on the assumption that large numbers allow other users to re-combine them to advantage).

As noted in Table 5, only a few surveys did not elicit information on occupation and most asked about several persons' occupation (respondent's, spouse's, etc.) and about other aspects of the subject (sector of employment, former occupations, etc.). On a few occasions, occupation was ascertained by means of a pre-coded question. This is an unsatisfactory procedure for most purposes, since neither respondents nor interviewers usually understand the relevant distinctions, and border-line decisions cannot be standardized across cases. In most instances, however, open-ended questions with various wordings were used. The best of these were probably those comprising several sub-questions or probes such as: 'What kind of work do you do? What is the name of your occupation and the title of your job?' Reminders to the interviewer to 'describe in detail' are also frequent. Coding was done according to many different schemes, some with only a few, some with very large numbers of categories. One of the most common schemes used was that devised by Bernard Blishen.[26] Some researchers interested in extensive coding used an adapted form of the U.S. Bureau of the Census classification, while a substantial number of the Centre de Sondage studies made use of the Statistics Canada code. *This latter scheme no doubt constitutes the best available solution at present, since it allows comparison with official statistics and facilitates collapsing of categories by means of scores in different columns. Though its complexity probably daunts many survey researchers, its disadvantages, we feel, are outweighed by flexibility and the possibility of comparison with Census and Labour Force studies.*

Table 6 seeks to give an idea of the frequency of occurrence of a few important distinctions in occupation and related questions. A few points are worth emphasizing.

For one thing the numbers refer, not to studies, but to instances when the variables were coded. In the English-lan-

Table 6
Types and Frequencies of Selected Occupational Categories and Distinctions
(number of instances)

Occupational categories	English	French
1. skilled-unskilled	49	62
2. blue-collar-white-collar	64	80
3. clerical	48	79
4. service occupations	32	35
5. supervisory	27	30
6. executive-managerial	22	73
7. professional	59	80
8. sales personnel	43	40
9. farmer	50	74

Other distinctions*	English	French
10. full vs. part time	4	34
11. ownership of business	34	17
12. self-employed	0	22
13. public-private domain	22	55
14. housewives	16	93
15. retired or pensioned	20	95
16. students	18	98
17. unemployed	25	95

*Some of the distinctions related to different aspects than occupation as such yield relatively higher scores because they are more frequently documented than are occupation codes.

guage studies, for example, although there were only 45 studies, occupation was coded 113 times, since separate codes were required when information was solicited about people other than respondent or head of household, and about jobs held at different times.

Second, some distinctions are clearly much more crucial than others. A separate category for farmers seems essential in rural or mixed populations, whereas one for sales personnel (within white collar) may not be for most purposes.

Third, of those studies which used the more concise occupation codes, only a few covered all the distinctions listed. Among English-language studies two cases made only one bifurcation, while most were in the range of four to six. The majority of French studies scored somewhat higher.

Taking complete occupation codes into account, not just the 17 distinctions singled out in Table 6, the median number of categories in English studies was 9 (including 'DK,' 'other,' etc.) with a range from 2 to 25. Most cases were near the median. In French studies (again excluding those using more complex codes such as Statistics Canada) the median was 11 but clustering around the median was even more marked. Where multiple-column scoring was employed, the individual columns were generally significant. (For example, a two-column code might have zero and one, for blue collar and white collar, in one column; and the other column would consist of distinctions within each of these two categories.)

Those data suggest a few very basic criteria about the coding of occupation which we recommend that scholars consider if an attempt, not possible here, is made to promote some standardization of this variable. *First, the largest possible number of primary categories is desirable,* both for the principal investigator and for secondary analysis. These can be easily machine re-coded into relevant typologies as needed. *Second, certain categories must be maintained.* Farmers are only one instance. Which categories may be significant will change in the long run, but some agreement should be feasible for any given decade. *Third, the question of compatibility between the existing widely used codes needs to be made the object of further research;* even the most detailed of codes still pose problems in this respect, often because they use conceptually different criteria. For example, the Statistics Canada code, while making most of the necessary distinctions within large categories, is based on a classification by economic sectors, while most of the shorter codes rely more upon the notion of specialization.[27]

Also, we feel that while there are no easy solutions to the problems involved in coding occupation, there are opportunities for improvement where the design of questions to ascertain occupation is concerned.

It is particularly important that researchers bear in mind that what is generally defined as 'occupation' involves in fact a series of interlocking questions, and not just one, if the research is to be sure of eliciting appropriate and adequate information for the needs of each study.

The sub-questions most frequently encountered are the following:

employment status
(employed, unemployed, retired, etc.)

occupational category of 'job'
(actual working activity)

sector of employment
(industrial sector, activity of employer)

ownership of business
(government, private enterprise, self-employed, etc.)

size of business
(number of employees, number of branches)

time basis
(part time, full time, etc.)

The above details are obviously not all necessary in all cases; only the first two are almost universally required. Equally they can be applied to a number of different working situations (present or previous jobs; main job or sideline) and to a number of different persons (respondent, head of household, father, etc.). However the *distinctions* between the different questions enumerated are essential, and failure to recognize them is very often a prime cause of inadequate information on 'occupation,' irrespective of the adequacy of the actual occupation codes used.

The decision on which of the above enumerated questions need to be asked, and about whom, is one that must be made in the light of the focus of each study. For some purposes respondent's occupation may be relevant; for others that of the head of household will suffice. In studies of career groups and students, respondent's occupation is known, and it may well be felt useful to enquire about respondent's father's occupation. When leisure activities are the focus of interest, secondary occupations will be important; when social mobility is a factor, former occupations must be ascertained; and so on.

Whatever the choice, however, investigators should attempt to ensure that the most basic relevant information will usually refer to the head of household's occupation, and frequently that of the respondent where different. However, in many cases the respondent may not be employed, so a certain amount of complex questioning must be used to ensure that some codable and pertinent 'occupation' is ascertained in all possible household situations. This entails separating questions on employment status from those on occupation as such. Failure to do this frequently results in 'retired,' 'housewife' or 'unemployed' being the only information available for analysis. Whatever the intrinsic interest of these responses, they do not serve the basic function of defining the social status either of the respondent or of the household.

The same rigorous distinctions between questions should be applied to other aspects of occupation. Aspects which are frequently confused are time basis (full or part time), employment status, and ownership of business. This leads to the use of unsatisfactory codes such as:

works part time
works full time
self-employed
housewife
student, etc.

The categories are clearly not mutually exclusive, since housewives and students often work part time, self-employed persons work either part time or full time, and so on. Instead of a single question, three separate ones should have been used: employment status (examples above), time basis (part time/full time), and ownership of business.

Another frequent source of confusion is the overlap between 'occupation' and 'sector of activity.' Even the most reputable coding schemes are not entirely devoid of this ambiguity. Here again the categories are not always mutually exclusive; for instance, 'office employees,' 'public servants,' 'skilled workers,' and 'transport and communications' are in the same 'occupation' code. It is often very useful to obtain information about the sector of employment and to use it as an aid to interpreting ambiguous job titles and descriptions; however in actual codes, the two should be kept systematically apart.

Sector of employment, like occupation, is usually ascertained by means of open-ended questions. For reasons similar to those given for occupation itself, this is the most satisfactory procedure. Follow-up questions and probes are also useful. A typical question would be: 'What sort of company or organization do you work for? What does the organization do?' with instructions to the interviewer to record full details. Some studies make doubly sure of getting the right definition by asking for the name and address of the organization involved which makes it possible to enquire directly or to use trade directories. A variety of coding schemes is used, ranging from the very concise to the elaborate. Among the latter the Statistics Canada code is probably the most flexible as well as lending itself to comparison with official statistics.

Finally a word about the simpler aspects of occupation, which pose few special problems other than those of confusion with other variables. 'Size of business' is often measured in addition to sector of employment. Generally the question refers to the number of employees, but care should be taken to specify in the question whether one intends the number of persons employed at the respondent's own place of work, or by the organization at large in a specified region. Generally the first alternative will provide more precise answers. In addition the number of sub-offices or branches in Canada can be as d. Actual numbers of course should be coded, or at least first digits of large numbers. 'Ownership of business' involves finding out whether respondent is self-employed or an employee of someone else. The question can also be used to ascertain whether the business or organization is privately or publicly owned. Occasionally the information required concerns ownership in ethnic terms — that is, whether the organization is Canadian-owned, American, European, Japanese, etc. All of these questions (especially about number of employees and ownership) may require information not possessed by respondents. Researchers should use such answers with due caution. Finally, 'time basis' usually means a question about whether the respondent is employed full or part time. For more precision one can ask and code the 'number of hours worked in an average week,' or hours per day and days per week.

Following are several forms which we recommend for ascertaining occupation in its many aspects. In every case, the questions may be adapted (with minor wording changes) for different individuals or time periods. Flashcards are useful for some questions in personal interviews.

Employment status of head of household

'What is the head of this household's current work situation? Is he (she) ....'

working for pay?
working without pay (e.g., in family business)?
Ask present *main occupation, below.*

unemployed?
temporarily laid off?
on strike?
Ask most recent *main occupation, below.*

retired or voluntarily inactive?
permanently disabled?
Ask former longest *occupation, below.*

keeping house?
a full time student?
Code as occupation; skip below.

Occupation of head of household[28]

'What type of work does the head of this household do (or did he/she do at his/her last job) (or did he/she do for most of his/her active life)?'

(*Probes*) 'What is (was) the name of his/her (main) occupation and the title of his/her job? What are (were) his/her duties? What does (did) he/she do exactly?'[29]

Sector of employment

'What sort of company or organization does the head of this household work for?'

(*Probes*) 'What does the company or organization *do*? What sort of product does it make, or what service does it render?'

Coding categories and coding manuals may both be obtained from Statistics Canada for these questions. The first two columns of the Statistics Canada occupational code indicate sector of employment. Furthermore, for summary purposes (since any given scholar will want only a few categories), the codes are fairly easily collapsible, with the qualifications noted above. Alternatively, the Blishen codes noted above can also be used for occupational prestige rankings, and they also facilitate the combining of adjacent categories.

Additional aspects which may interest some scholars are outlined here:

Ownership of business

'Who does that company or organization belong to? Is it a private company belonging to someone else? Is it his own company or business? Or is it a federal, provincial, or municipal government agency? Or what?'

private company belonging to someone else
own company or business
federal agency
provincial agency
municipal agency
other non-profit agency
other (*specify*)

Alternative

Ownership of business

'Is (head) self-employed or does he work for someone else?'
self-employed
works for someone else

Size of company or organization

'How many branches or plants does this company or organization have in (Canada/this province/this city/etc.)?'
Number:

'How many people work in the same branch or plant as (head)?'
Number:

Alternative

Size of company or organization

'How many people does this company or organization employ altogether in (Canada/this province/this city/etc.)?'
Number:

Time basis

'How many hours does (head) usually work each week?'
Number of hours:

Alternative

Time basis

'Does (head) work full time or part time?'
full time
part time

In the questions on size of company and time basis, actual numeric codes can be used or first digits can be coded.

Income

Under the general heading of income also, several types of information are generated. Some studies ask about family income, others only about respondent's; most query 'last year's income,' some specify 'this year's.' A few even ask about parents' income. There are, of course, theoretical perspectives from which one finds each of these types of income a necessary object of enquiry. For comparative equivalence, however, a 'core' question would be desirable. Additional questions could then be asked, as they are now, having a more specialized focus. From a statistical point of view, the most common question concerns a household or family's total gross income (before deductions or tax) last year. For household-based surveys this would no doubt serve most purposes, so long as the respondent (often a student or housewife) was able to make an educated guess. Individual income or salary will of course be more relevant for most individual-based studies. In some respects, *sources* of income may be important, since as indicators of status, different types of income may be accorded differential prestige.

It is reassuring that the overwhelming majority of studies ascertained income. The lack of specificity, however, is disconcerting. For example, a majority of studies do not specify the year for which an estimate is desired; some specify 'this year's income,' and others ask about 'last year's.' There is sometimes confusion about total income from all sources vs. salary and wages; likewise about gross or net of taxes and deductions. Family or household vs. individual must be specified, but this is not done regularly.[30] Also interviewers must, of course, be in a position to give guarantees of confidentiality, and in specific circumstances it may be desirable to write this into the question.

We recommend that the basic question elicit information on:

last year's
family or household income
from all sources
before taxes and deductions

unless there are compelling reasons not to do so because of special theoretical needs or peculiar characteristics of the sample population (e.g., students). One special need concerns telephone interviews which may not be able to get such detailed information. More than likely, the problem here will involve 1)reading out a reduced number of fairly broad categories and 2)more specific reassurances about refusal to divulge such data.

The majority of studies ascertained income by means of a closed-ended question and flashcard. The Survey Research Centre, York University, frequently uses a device designed to save the respondent from the embarrassment of having to quote a figure, or a numeric code resembling one; random letter codes are provided whereby the respondent can designate the appropriate category.[31] A worthwhile safety precaution also used by the Survey Research Centre involves the addition of a follow-up question: 'Does that include the income of everyone living here?' ensuring that global household income is actually ascertained.[32]

Since pre-coding is so common, most of the variation in coding schemes concerns the number and width of categories. The median and modal number of categories turns out to be a respectable nine, in both English and French-language studies, with the range being 4 to 20. Except for the lowest category (which is usually 'under $1000,' 'under $2000,' or 'under $4000' per year), the category widths are almost always either $1000 or $2000 intervals. The highest category, of course, is open: above a certain amount ($10,000 and $15,000 being the most common).[33]

Therefore, a degree of standardization can be inferred. Although there is no agreement on the type of income about which the respondent is questioned, coding is fairly regular. One can conclude that a norm of $1000 or $2000 intervals has developed, with a moderately high upper category. Given inflation and growing affluence, it would probably be useful to have a category of 'over $25,000' or 'over $30,000' rather than the more common ones mentioned above. The most frequently used breakdowns are listed below.

For personal interviews we recommend the following question (and follow-up) in conjunction with a flashcard listing the income categories.

Household income

'Looking at this card, could you tell me which category comes closest to the total income of all the members of this household for last year (19..), before tax and deductions?'

less than $2000
2000 to 2999
3000 to 3999
4000 to 4999
5000 to 5999
6000 to 6999
7000 to 7999
8000 to 8999
9000 to 9999
10,000 to 11,999
12,000 to 14,999
15,000 to 19,999
20,000 to 29,999
30,000 and more

(*Follow-up*)

"Does this total include *all* sources of income and *everyone* in this household who works?'

yes

no
(*Correct above total.*)

For telephone interviews, it may be advisable to substitute the following question, adapted for unusually high or low income groups as dictated by the sampling procedures.

Household income

'What approximately was your household's total income last year (19..), before taxes and deductions? Was it....'

less than $6000?
between $6000 and $8999?
between $9000 and $11,999?
$12,000 and more?

(*Follow-up*)

'Does that total include *all* sources of income and *everyone* who works?'

yes

no
(*Correct above total.*)

Education

The most commonly asked question, education in some respects displays a degree of standardization. Two main forms of the question exist, one asking years of schooling, the other levels and types of education received. The former was found to be somewhat more frequent than the latter. In many cases years of schooling were combined, reducing the value of the variable for re-analysis purposes. Most studies which did this endeavoured to make the categories coincide with the average number of years required to complete the various programs of education (e.g., 0-8 for primary education, and so on); others did not even do this and adopted five-year intervals which cut across the traditionally significant boundaries. *We recommend that all of the exact years completed be directly coded.*

About half the studies ascertained level of education as well as years, while a number used the former question alone. The coding of this information was the source of much variation, because of differences in breakdown by province, by country of origin, and over time, and because of the number of additional qualifications, with varying degrees of specialization, which may be acquired outside the regular school system. Some researchers felt it preferable to leave the question open and decide about equivalence of diplomas in coding. For certain highly specialized populations, this is probably feasible, but for general population samples it is a laborious process and most researchers leave it up to respondents and interviewers to pick the most appropriate category from a pre-coded list. The minimum distinctions made are those between primary, secondary and post-secondary education. Many studies also distinguish between programs which were completed or not completed and some add varying numbers of categories to cover post-secondary, non-university diplomas (teaching diplomas, business school, etc.). Difficulties arise with these coding schemes in cases where the different provincial (and foreign) education systems do not have the same cut-off points. Such problems involve the Quebec CEGEPs and classical colleges and New Brunswick Junior High Schools, for instance. Obviously, codes must be designed to meet the needs of specific samples, but we give a few common examples below. *Generally speaking, number of years plus a question on the highest level of education attained would seem to be the most adequate way of covering the subject, each of the two questions allowing for some interpretation of the meaning of the other.*

Other potential problems face secondary users of this variable. For one thing, the school leaving age and the number of years required for secondary school graduation vary by province, by generation, and by country of origin. A sensitive analyst can account for these if he is careful, especially when the survey ascertains other variables such as country or province of childhood, age, and special training programs. Nevertheless, scholars could be more meticulous about these matters than they are. Second, as education becomes more common, the attainment of any given level of formal schooling up to post-secondary is a less reliable indicator of class or status. Scholars must, hence, be cautious in using education as a control variable when comparing age cohorts. Finally, these strictures may apply mainly to education as a measure of status. When it is conceptualized as a direct cause of attitudes, values, and beliefs, on the other hand, different problems arise.

From the material we have examined it is also worth remarking that education is used as a more 'individualized' variable than other indicators of status. In a large number of studies respondent's level (or years) of education is the only question asked. Where supplementary questions are included, they concern the educational level attained by the respondent's parents or spouse. Only very rarely is the education of the head of household asked for specifically. It would appear therefore that income (household's or head's) and occupation (of head of household) are most frequently used to define household status, while education is used almost invariably to define respondent's status, backed up by respondent's occupation and, more infrequently, respondent's personal income.

As a final observation, we may note that studies which omit the variable 'education' are often those using student samples in which the level of education is known to investigators. *While education is clearly of less use in defining status in the case of student samples, it is nonetheless reasonable to recommend, once again, that the level of the students sampled be documented.*

We recommend that both of the following questions be asked and coded. The exact years should be coded in the first case, and in the second these distinctions should be maintained as the minimum acceptable categories. With specialized samples (immigrants, professionals, etc.) or in certain provinces, additional subdivisions are advisable.

'How many years of schooling have you completed altogether?'

Number:

'What was the highest level of schooling you reached?'

some primary school
completed primary school
some high school
completed high school
technical training beyond high school
college or some university
graduated from university
other (*specify*)

Social Class

Two basically different techniques fall under this heading — interviewer assessment of class or respondent's own self-identification. Generally, if an interviewer assesses class, it is a judgment about household status on the basis of observed material possessions (type of housing, furniture, type of books and magazines). As such it differs sharply from (although it is correlated with) self-assessment or identification. This is mentioned only to point out that some indicator of 'class' may be present, and hence available for re-analysis, even if the respondent was never asked.

The two forms can easily be coded together, so that anomalous cases can be identified, though this is rare now. (If both are coded, the interviewer may have been biased in making the assessment by the respondent's stated class identification.)

When asked to specify his class, the respondent is almost always confronted with a pre-coded set of categories. Variety arises from the number and labelling of categories. For example, there may be a 'middle class' or a middle and 'lower middle' class, a 'working' or a working and 'lower' class. Though these terms relate to somewhat different concepts, they can nearly always be regrouped into upper, middle, and lower, if a researcher wishes.

Class is a difficult concept for Canadians to comprehend. Probes are, therefore, fairly common. The most frequent is to respond to a denial of class affiliation by asking the respondent his class if there were such things. The whole set of categories also presents translation problems. The notions of 'upper,' 'middle' and 'lower' class have long been familiar to English-speaking North-Americans; even if an anglophone Canadian refuses to place himself in any class, he attaches some kind of meaning to the question. Although literal translations can of course be found, French-speaking respondents have grave problems identifying with any of the categories, since these do not seem to correspond to the way they view social differences.[34] Indeed, 'class' was present in only three of the 81 'French' questionnaires examined.

The median and modal number of classes coded is 5, the range being from 2 to 8. From this one can infer that either 'middle' or 'lower' class (or both) has been subdivided in most cases.

It is clear that a great deal of uniformity exists, suggesting a fairly clear norm among researchers. Despite this, we have discussed this variable here rather than in the previous section for the sake of comparison with other variables in the 'status cluster.' However it should be added that direct questions about 'class,' whether addressed to respondent or to interviewer, fulfil a different function from the other indicators of social status we have discussed and cannot be considered a direct substitute for these or as a short-cut around the problems posed by defining and coding occupation or education. What precise

meaning respondents attach to the notion of class is a
matter for debate. An interviewer's judgment will of
course be affected by his own class background. Therefore
if an *objective* assessment of class is what is required, researchers must evaluate and choose from among the various more reliable indicators of social status which have
been developed.

We recommend the following questions, with additional
categories for specialized (elite) samples. The wording
may, of course, be adapted to ascertain the social class of
other persons (head, father, etc.). The third question is
less pertinent and reliable than the others.

'People often think of themselves as belonging to one social class or another. Most people say they belong to the
upper-middle class, the middle class, or the working class.
Do you ever think of yourself as belonging to a social
class?'

Yes

No

Don't know

'If you had to make a choice, would you call yourself upper-middle class, middle class, working class, or what?'

Upper-middle class

Middle class

Working class

Other (*specify*)

No such thing

Don't know

'In what class do you think most other people would place
you?'

Upper-middle class

Middle class

Working class

Other (*specify*)

No such thing

Don't know

Properties of the Status Cluster

We have indicated that where the particular variable of interest to a scholar is absent, it may be possible to substitute another variable even though it measures a different facet of status than the first. This is certainly the case with the four variables just discussed. Fifteen of the 45 English-language studies, for example, measured all four variables; 18 more measured three; and several measured two. Only three French schedules measured all four variables (the virtual absence of 'class' from the French material being the reason for this), while 45 out of 81 included three out of four; another 31 measured two and two measured only one. At least one of the four was to be found in every study, in whichever language, although, as has been mentioned earlier, the way the variables are measured sometimes leaves much to be desired. This cluster, however, unlike other clusters, poses almost no barrier to secondary analysis in terms of availability of material, provided a researcher is in a position to substitute one variable for another. We hasten to add, however, that the possibility of substituting one member of the cluster for another, while a valuable aid in the absence of one's preferred variable, in no way diminishes the need to standardize these variables further. Furthermore, the reader must bear in mind the theoretical and technical problems involved in substitution which we mentioned above.

IX The Ethnicity-Religion Cluster

Grave difficulties, apart from standardization, confront the analyst of ethnicity. Some of these conceptual problems have been pointed out in earlier works.[35] We shall only mention them here as a warning to secondary users of these variables.

There is general agreement that ancestral origins are a relatively unreliable source of classification into ethnic groups, at least for many purposes. They mask the facts that a)political boundaries change, and in any event b)political boundaries have never delimited ethnically homogeneous populations, while at the same time c)immigrants to Canada are likely to be drawn disproportionately from minority ethnic groups in their country of origin (for example, Mennonites from Germany or Russia).

Language appears to offer more solid foundations for classification, but people are often bilingual or multilingual, requiring a judgment about the operational measurement of 'mother tongue.' Some studies ascertain the language of childhood, home, work, friendship, and worship. There is no perfect correlation among incidences of these uses of language, and in many contexts the results produced may differ very widely indeed.

Respondent's self-identification of ethnicity, while more accurate for certain purposes, poses a problem of classification since it can be variously phrased. Furthermore, such identification can be inaccurate, as the case of 'Pennsylvania Dutch' (actually German) demonstrates. Equally vexing is the frequent response of 'Canadian' as one's ethnic identity.

Religion is quite revealing for certain groups but less so for others. Mennonites or Hindus will turn out to be ethnically distinct; Protestants and Catholics much less so. The reasons for this derive from the varying degrees to which religion is correlated with the other dimensions just mentioned (especially language).

Race might be of some use in ethnic research, but not in most Canadian communities at present. As noted earlier, it is virtually never asked. Furthermore, it is an ambiguous concept, though for different reasons, to both scholars and respondents. Consider the differences between racial identification and race as a 'gene pool.' For many people, racial differences are found only among non-whites;

whereas among 'white' races, ethnic differences are emphasized.

Probably the surest course for proper identification of ethnic groups in survey research involves multiple classification by two or more of the above characteristics. Therefore, after discussing each variable, we shall present data on the incidence of clustering in our surveys.

Religion

In this report we focus on religious affiliation or background, ignoring religious behaviour (such as church attendance) or devoutness (as an attitude or ideology). These latter variables are, of course, important in many contexts, but not for purposes of socio-demographic classification or ethnicity. However, the realization that they do occur frequently in conjunction with religious affiliation (well over half the surveys examined which asked about religion also included some measure of behaviour or devoutness) is helpful in interpreting the choice of questions and of codes for this variable. It indicates, notably, that researchers do not always perceive 'religion' primarily as an ethnic variable.

As Table 5 revealed, about half the surveys questioned respondents about their religious affiliation, and several asked the religion of head of household, spouse, parents, etc. No type of survey consistently omitted this question, though it seems less frequent in those dealing with employment or career groups. When asked, the norm clearly favours a closed, pre-coded question, though usually with an opportunity for specification of an 'other' category.

Almost all coding schemes provide separate categories for Roman Catholic, Jewish, and Protestant. Among two-thirds of the French-language studies examined, these were the only religions listed, though about half the English studies provided space for Greek Orthodox and other Eastern religions. Nearly all schemes coded as separate the response 'no religion,' and some made elaborate distinctions between categories of non-believers. All in all, the median number of coding categories in English-language studies is 9 (though 10 is the mode), which indicates also that Protestant is generally subdivided. (How it is subdivided varies greatly. There is a clear tendency to ask for exact Protestant sect or denomination, but to code these as only a few categories.) Among French-language surveys in Quebec, the median is considerably lower at 6, since less subdivision of the Protestant category occurs, and fewer other religions are mentioned at all, particularly the orthodox religions which seem under-represented.

Most studies choose to ascertain religious affiliation by means of a question about current religion, phrased variously as 'What is your religion?', 'What is your religious preference?', etc. These different versions probably yield differing response rates in terms of actual religions cited, but for a researcher interested in religion as an ethnic indicator they are all likely to produce too many 'none' responses, given present day trends towards agnosticism and non-denominational religions. A more productive question may well be religious background or religion of childhood — 'In what religion were you raised as a child?' for example, or, alternatively, parents' religion, though this will create problems in 'mixed' marriages.

For most purposes, we therefore recommend either or both of the following questions.

Current religious affiliation

'What is your religion?'[36]

None
Anglican
Baptist
Greek Orthodox
Jewish
Lutheran
Mennonite
Pentecostal
Presbyterian
Roman Catholic
Salvation Army
Ukrainian Catholic
United Church
Other (*specify*)

Religious background, or religion of childhood, may be ascertained by asking about parental religious practice or respondent's childhood religious affiliation. The same coding conventions as above should be employed, again adapted to special target populations if necessary.

'What was your parents' religious preference (religion) when you were growing up?'

or

'What was your religious preference (religion) when you were growing up?'

Language

Language is measured in all types of surveys at about an equal rate (rather more than half). Most common are precoded questions, but open-ended questions are to be found in a few cases.

Variety arises, first of all, in whether the language coded is spoken as 'first language,' at home, at work, or in the interview. Although there is some positive correlation among these types, not all are equally reliable for general purposes. Language of work is, of course, influenced by the working context, and economically weak linguistic groups are absorbed into the economically dominant groups. Language of interview is affected by the linguistic affiliation of the interviewer as well as that of the respondent. Both variables are of interest, and language of interview should certainly be coded, but not as a basic indicator of respondent's ethnicity.

Choice of a single question poses a dilemma. If 'mother tongue' is chosen, this enhances the usefulness of language as an indicator of ethnicity (since it refers to one's background).[37] Language used 'at home' is less useful for background but more so for current usage of 'identification.'

Both are now comparable with census data and we recommend that both be recorded whenever feasible. Census forms of the questions should be used for increased comparability.

A disconcerting number of studies currently rely on 'French/English/other' as a coding scheme. Occasionally

English-language studies have a category 'non-European languages.' *It would seem reasonable to suggest that a list of, say, the 10 most common languages in the province or city where the study is conducted be used for studies covering linguistically heterogeneous populations. Some languages which are particularly valuable as ethnic indicators, such as Yiddish and certain non-European languages, should be added to the list where appropriate.*

Mother tongue[38]

'What is your mother tongue, that is, the first language you spoke which you still understand?'

English
French
German
Ukrainian
Italian
Dutch
Polish
A Native language (Indian or Inuit)
A Scandinavian language
Magyar
Yiddish
Other (*specify*)

Language most used at home

'What language do you most often speak at home now?'

Language of schedule or questionnaire

May be pre-coded on the printed instrument, usually at end, e.g.:

Language of questionnaire
☑   English

Language of interview

When language of interview may be different from the above (i.e., when interpreters are used), an additional question to the interviewer is required:

'In what language was the interview conducted?'

For the last three questions, the same coding scheme should be used as for mother tongue.

Nativity

All types of surveys examined code nativity (in some sense) in similar rates, and this is usually done by means of a closed question containing from one to 38 categories, with a median of 7 for English-language studies. In all cases where asked, respondent's country of birth (or early childhood) is the object of questioning, and in about a third of the cases this is also ascertained for father, mother, or both. Spouse's origin is also sometimes asked.

Among English-language studies the almost universal coding categories include Canada, United States, United Kingdom, and one or more European countries (equally divided between more and less than 7). About a third of the English-language coding schemes have one or more categories for Asian countries. French-language studies examined used substantially fewer categories, one third being content with 'Canada/elsewhere' as a breakdown.

In addition to country of origin, about two thirds of the English studies which ask about nativity also provide data on the year (or period) of immigration. This question was not found frequently among French-language studies. Relatively rare in both languages are questions about citizenship, and also information about the number of generations resident in Canada. Some English-language studies query province of origin, if born in Canada; a fairly substantial number of Quebec studies use this breakdown, or even finer ones concerning regions of Quebec while making no distinction among countries outside Canada.

We cannot recommend a single list of countries which should be pre-coded. Instead we recommend the following options:

1)for national surveys, use the 10 most common countries among immigrants according to the latest census, taking a national average;

2)for a survey in one or more provinces (or a single city), use the 10 most common countries of origin for the relevant geographic unit(s) sampled;

3)always have a category 'other';

4)the survey's purpose may determine whether Britain is a satisfactory category, or whether it should be subdivided (England, Scotland, etc.); this also seems to depend on where the survey is conducted.

Ethnic Self-Identification and Ethnic Origin

These variables are fairly common in most types of surveys and, while closed formats are more frequent, open-ended questions are also to be found. Although many of the categories coincide with those used to code country of birth, ethnicity itself tends to produce more detailed coding; the median category number among English-language studies was 14 with a range from 2 to 38. The extra category most frequently encountered was Jewish, followed by native Indians and Inuit, and Chinese and Japanese.

Two distinct (though somewhat related) dimensions are encompassed by this variable, ethnic origin (as defined by the Census)[39] and current subjective identification. Both have merits and defects as basic background variables, and it is therefore difficult to recommend one over the other. The former approach, by referring back to a historical fact, reduces the likelihood of 'Canadian' as a response, and it has the advantage of comparability with Census data. However, it generates fairly high 'don't know' rates among long established rural populations, particularly in Quebec, and tends elsewhere to group into the same category new immigrants with persons whose origins are so far removed that they have little chance of predicting distinctive attitudinal and behavioural patterns. Subjective identification on the other hand produces 'Canadian' responses (which may be an accurate measure of assimilation in some cases, but a reflection of the will to assimilate in others). It also creates awkward combinations like 'Canadian Italian' vs. 'Italian Canadian' vs. 'Canadian of Italian descent.' These pose interviewing problems if closed-ended questions are used (the interviewer needs a quick eye to pick out the correct one) as well as 'readability' problems in French. Moreover, narrowing down the list to single-barrelled categories, or instructing the interviewer not to accept 'Canadian' as a response, does not entirely remove the problem, since ethnic identification is something people feel strongly about and they will refuse to identify with what they consider inappropriate labels.

A few studies attempt to bypass the choice by asking questions like 'What is your ethnic origin?' or 'To what ethnic group do you belong?', which generate problems of their own, 'ethnic origin' being a somewhat learned term, and 'ethnic group' being frequently understood to designate groups other than English and French. A number also supplement the question on paternal ancestors by asking about maternal ancestors too. Serious consideration should be given to use of the Statistics Canada questions, instructions, and coding procedures given below.

Regardless of the choice between these different approaches we recommend that the precise meaning of the question be made clear, and that a standard list be drawn up according to the frequency of the various groups in the city or region where the study is to be conducted. Especially significant groups should be included whenever appropriate (e.g., Jewish, Indian, Inuit, etc.).

Ethnic origin (by male ancestors)[40]

'To what ethnic or cultural group did you or your ancestor (on the male side) belong on coming to this continent?'

British[41]
Irish
French
German
Ukrainian
Italian
Dutch
Scandinavian
Jewish
Russian
Other (*specify*)

Ethnic self-identification

'Apart from being Canadian, to what ethnic or cultural
group do you consider yourself to belong?'

British[41]
Irish
French
German
Ukrainian
Italian
Dutch
Scandinavian
Jewish
Russian
Native Indian or Inuit
'Just Canadian'
Québecois
Other (*specify*)

Properties of the Ethnicity-Religion Cluster

Unlike the status cluster, the dimensions within ethnicity
are neither so prevalent nor so jointly common. There are
several studies which ascertain none of the four variables,
or only one low significance variable (e.g., religion alone).
In many cases, however, this is either because these
studies are conducted among ethnically homogeneous
populations or because ethnic criteria were used for sampling. Combinations of variables differ widely from one
study to another, language in one form or another being
the most common and the one most frequently used on its
own.

We may tentatively conclude from this that most researchers consider language to be the single most significant indicator of ethnicity. Its precision can, of course, be
greatly improved by the addition of one or more of the
other three. However, the usefulness of any one of the others on its own in the general context of ethnicity is more
questionable, for reasons already mentioned. *We recommend, therefore, the inclusion of language as a basic
'ethnicity' question, supplemented by the other three
whenever possible. We also strongly urge more detailed
coding in order that all of these questions may be used as*

sources of information on ethnicity even when the primary investigator does not intend to use them as such. This entails not being content with singling out one or two very broad categories and grouping all the rest under 'other,' as is frequently done. It also involves research on the most likely categories to be of use in a given geographical or social context.

Table 7
The Ethnicity Cluster

Frequency of occurence by date of survey and by language	1960's			1970's			Total*
	English	French	Total	English	French	Total	
religion/language/ nativity/ethnicity	9	1	10	3	8	11	23
religion/language/ ethnicity	2	1	3	1	4	5	8
religion/language/ nativity	1	1	2	0	3	3	5
religion/ethnicity/ nativity	1	0	1	3	1	4	5
language/ethnicity/ nativity	0	2	2	0	2	2	4
language/nativity	2	1	3	0	3	3	6
religion/language	2	1	3	0	7	7	10
religion/ethnicity	2	0	2	1	0	1	3
religion/nativity	2	0	2	1	1	2	4
language/ethnicity	0	0	0	0	3	3	3
language/nativity	0	1	1	0	0	0	1
religion only	1	2	3	1	2	3	7
language only	0	1	1	2	11	13	14
nativity only	0	1	1	3	2	5	7
ethnicity only	0	3	3	0	3	3	8
none of the four	0	7	7	3	7	10	18
*Totals	22	22	44	18	57	75	126

* Totals exceed other columns because a few surveys could not be dated from available information.

X The Political Party Cluster

Although political party membership may be treated as an instance of organizational affiliation, and hence was implicitly dealt with in an earlier section, two decades of research on this cluster of variables demonstrates the importance of separate analysis.[42] Several features of party affiliation reveal its distinctive status. First, 'membership' in a party is rarely a clear-cut matter in Canada, as it is with trade union membership. It is more akin to church affiliation — as much a matter of emotion or attendance as of formal 'joining.' This is particularly true of the two major parties. Second, activity tends to be extremely sporadic, peaking in the weeks before an election and being virtually non-existent otherwise. Third, 'party identification' or 'feeling close to' a party seems to have consequences similar to the formal membership more characteristic of other organizations.

There is, of course, debate among social scientists about the nature of party affiliation and the generalizability of concepts and conclusions from one party system to another. Nevertheless, this controversy requires data to resolve it, and time series data have begun and should be carried forward. Therefore, in this section we look at three common techniques for measuring the kind and degree of 'membership' in political parties. As Table 5 demonstrated, each of the three occurs in about one quarter of the studies examined here, though they are most common in election studies, public opinion polls, and student opinion surveys.

The three variables are: degree of activity in support of a party; partisanship or party identification; and voting history or intentions. They are positively intercorrelated in empirical studies, and they tend to co-occur in the same types of surveys; studies either examine the subject in some detail or ignore it completely.

Partisan Activity

Although the least frequently measured variable in the cluster, degree of activity on behalf of a political party is in some ways the most informative. To mention one's adherence to a party is one thing; to work actively is quite another.

An interesting feature is that most surveys asking about

this variable do not ask which party the respondent supports, only whether or not he supports one. This may stem
from the fact that when this question is asked there is
almost always another question on voting for or identification with a particular party. *If used alone, we recommend that it be supplemented by asking which party a
respondent supports.*

A serious complexity concerns the notion of membership.
For most federal parties, there is no formal membership,
in the sense of regular dues or carrying a card. For some
provincial parties, and for some provincial or federal riding associations, membership is formalized, but not for all,
as far as we know. Furthermore, we are unclear how to
count, for membership purposes, a college or university
party club. It seems advisable, therefore, not to try to develop a general question on membership at this time. Depending on sampling and on specific theoretical needs,
each scholar can devise those best suited to elicit the precise information needed. Nevertheless, we do urge investigators interested in this area to explore various alternatives, including the relative importance of different types
of membership and types of activity. Until considerably
more work has been done, however, the following suggestions may be tentatively offered.

Extent of activity in support of a political party[43]

'Do you attend meetings organized by a political party or
do voluntary work for it? Which party is that?'
Yes
No
Name of party:

'Is that a federal or provincial organization?'
Federal
Provincial
Other

'In an average month (year), how many hours would you
say you spend at these meetings or doing voluntary work
for the party?'
Number of hours:

'Do you hold any kind of office within the party organization or serve on any committees?'

No

Yes

'What exactly is that? What do you do?'

We cannot suggest any standard coding scheme for this last question. More experience is needed with the relevant populations.

'Have you ever contributed financial support to a political party?'

No

Yes

'Which party was that?'

Same coding scheme as for party identification below.

'Was that federally or provincially?'

Federal

Provincial

Both

Other

If respondent has contributed to more than one party, separate codes are needed.

Party Identification

As measured for two decades in a number of countries, this variable consists of responses to questions about the party which a respondent 1)habitually supports, or 2)'feels closest to,' or 3)'thinks of himself' as a member of. It is invariably a measure of psychological attachment, and as such does not strictly speaking fall within the domain of sociodemographic variables we set ourselves. It has been included, however, to round out the set of variables in this section.

There has been some dispute among survey specialists about the wording best suited to tap this variable, and which of the above three facets to emphasize; but some uniformities have developed. It is asked mainly in election studies, public opinion polls, and studies of student opinions. When asked, it is almost always a pre-coded set of closed categories (except for a category 'other'). Occasionally a flashcard is employed or a 'feeling thermometer.'

The median number of categories coded falls between 6 and 7 with a range of 4 to 35. The modal number is 5. Classifications vary by province; most common on the federal level are Liberal, Progressive Conservative, and New Democratic Party (or CCF), with Social Credit (Creditiste) almost as frequent. Very common categories include 'no partisan allegiance' and 'other party'; and many other parties (such as Communist) with declining freqency.

There has been confusion in some surveys about the referents of identification, whether federal or provincial parties. We therefore recommend that two questions be asked, one for each level, or that, if only one level is asked, both the questions and the code book be unambiguous about which level was intended. Without strong feelings about the exact wording, we nevertheless urge scholars to include questions such as the following (with appropriate substitutions of the word 'provincial' for 'federal,' and of provincial party names according to province):

'Thinking of (federal) politics, do you usually think of yourself as (Liberal, Conservative, NDP, Social Credit, or what)?'
Liberal
Progressive Conservative
NDP
Social Credit
Other party (*specify*)
Independent (sometimes one, sometimes another)
No partisan allegiance (rejects all parties)
Don't know

'Still thinking of federal politics, do you ever think of yourself as being a little closer to one of the parties than to the others?' (*If yes*) 'Which one is that?'
Yes, Liberal
Yes, Progressive Conservative

Yes, NDP
Yes, Social Credit
Yes, other party (*specify*)
Yes, but don't know which
No
Don't know

Obviously, the list of parties used in coding will have to be adapted depending on the province and on the population sampled. Ideally, scholars might also ask about the strength of identification and about previous identifications if changes have occurred. If these aspects are probed, the questions should follow immediately after the above queries, and they should also indicate clearly whether federal or provincial level is intended.

Voting Record

This variable is somewhat more widely distributed across type of surveys than the previous two, though still most common in election and public opinion surveys. It almost invariably takes the form of a pre-coded, closed question with five or six categories (the median is 6, mode is 5, range of 2 to 17). The categories, needless to say, are quite similar to those for party identification.

The near uniformity of format for question and coding masks variety as to the election to which the question is directed. These elections may be federal or provincial, the current election, previous election, second previous one, or the next election. Frequently also the authors of studies carried out in non-election periods ask about what party respondents would vote for 'if an election were to be held tomorrow.' These distinctions make no difference in principle, but scholars using data sets for re-analysis must be clear about the referent; otherwise confusion can result from combining distributions for quite different elections or levels. For the sake of clarity, *we therefore recommend that for this variable as for all others, the exact question, as asked, be included in the code book.*

We also recommend, of course, that the same basic categories be used here as for the questions on party identification. Additional categories should perhaps be added for people who were not eligible to vote during the election to which the question refers, for those who cast blank ballots, and another for those who did not vote.

'In talking about the (federal) election which was held in (month/year), we find that a lot of people were not able to vote because they were sick, or didn't have time, or for some other reason. How about you? Did you vote or did something keep you from voting?'

Voted
Did not vote
Don't remember

'For which party did you vote?'
Liberal
Progressive Conservative
NDP
Social Credit
Other party (*specify*)
Cast blank ballot
Not eligible to vote
Don't remember
Refused to say

Properties of the Political Party Cluster

One of the main purposes of examining sets of variables in the context of a cluster concerns their substitutability. In other words, can a researcher find a 'second best' variable out of the cluster if his preferred variable was not asked? In the case of status variables, we found the answer to be 'yes'; and in the case of ethnicity there were only a few surveys that failed to measure any of the variables. In the case of political party support, however, substitutability is less common. Nearly 40 per cent of the surveys, for example, asked about none of these three variables. Generally, if one was asked, a second or even a third was common.

The explanation for the difference between the clusters in this respect stems, we feel, from the popularity of certain theoretical perspectives in Canadian social science. The widespread interest in class (and related role variables) has engendered a presumption that one or more status variables will always be present in surveys. Similarly, the official status of bilingualism and multiculturalism predisposes scholars to enquire about language, religion, and ethnicity. Party affiliation, though an influential variable, has not attracted such widespread interest. This may be due to the recency of research on party identification, compared to class analysis or the study of French-English relations. It may also stem from the fact that party is often a dependent variable whereas the others are more commonly viewed (sometimes mistakenly) as independent variables. When party vote or identification is accorded independent causal status, its predictive powers are usually explored only for political attitude variables. It is hoped that this report will encourage an exploration of broader perspectives.

XI Loss of Information

At several points in this report we have referred to the problem of loss of information at various stages of the survey process. Such loss is as great a hindrance to the use of data for secondary analysis as lack of standardization, and requires less study to correct in many instances. For this reason we have thought it useful to devote a short section of the report to a recapitualtion of the principal causes of loss of information.

Poor documentation is undoubtedly a serious and widespread problem. In order to accumulate material on socio-economic variables, code books were obviously the main source of information to which we had to gain access. Not all studies have code books, however, and in such cases the interview schedule had to be used instead. Of course, interview schedules only contain codes for closed-ended questions, and even then not all codes may have been foreseen. Key variables like occupation often remain undocumented. Code books, when available, are not always much more informative. Actual question texts are often missing, as are special instructions to interviewers. Cover sheet information and ID codes are not always explained. Even the date of the study and name of the investigator are sometimes absent. Coding schemes may also be incomplete, pointing to ill-coordinated coding operations where individuals were at liberty to invent new codes without documenting them for the use of others. When both schedules and code books are available, it is often apparent that important questions were asked and then not coded at all, presumably for lack of time or money or expertise. This occurs particularly frequently with occupation, sector of employment, and level of education, among the variables we have looked at, and is also a common problem with open-ended attitudinal questions.

Although we were not specifically looking for other types of documentation, it also seemed clear that had we wished to consult sampling and field reports on the various studies we examined we would have encountered even more difficulties. Yet these constitute minimum documentation for anyone doing secondary analysis. It would seem reasonable that funding agencies require grant recipients to submit, in addition to reports, a complete set of technical documents upon termination of projects: schedules and other field instruments, sampling reports containing weighting information if relevant, and of course adequate code books. Funds should, of course, be allocated and used specifically for these purposes.

In the design and processing of the survey instrument itself we have pointed to several frequent sources of loss of information. One of these was failure to include key variables when these were not seen as useful for short-term primary analysis purposes. A second cause was failure to cover the most useful aspect of a variable, as when status is measured solely by interviewer evaluation, or language by language of interview. A third factor was inappropriate pre-coding of certain questions leading to loss of information between respondent and interviewer. Examples of this (irretrievable) loss of information were pre-coded numeric variables (age, length of residence, number of children, etc.) and pre-coded categories in complex variables such as occupation which, besides 'losing' information, rendered what information was collected highly unreliable. In making this criticism we do not, of course, wish to imply that pre-coding responses in general is an undesirable practice. On the contrary, a researcher who has done adequate groundwork and pretesting before finalizing his instrument and who has a coherent plan for analyzing his data once they are collected, will normally be in a position to 'close' all but a very few questions. However, those questions which call for conceptually complex judgments in coding must be left to specially trained personnel working in conditions which make standardized borderline judgments feasible, and must not be coded by interviewer or respondent.

Loss of information is also frequent at the ensuing stage of the survey operation, that is, in coding. The overall result is about the same as when pre-coded categories are used: 1)information which could have been recorded in sufficient detail to be re-grouped according to different criteria for re-analysis is forced into too few categories or categories which are appropriate only for limited purposes, and 2)when altogether too few categories have been used, extreme heterogeneity is to be found within each category. This type of loss, while serious, may in some cases be remedied more easily than loss through pre-coding provided the original schedules are kept for subsequent re-coding. But this, of course, should be considered as a last resort once the harm is done, not as acceptable procedure, because of the duplication of effort it involves.

The type of loss encountered, and the extent of the loss,
differs with individual variables. Some, as we have mentioned, are simply not included as often as they might be;
those relating to political parties, organizational membership, residential mobility, and household composition are
examples. Others are almost universally asked; but failure
to ask the most relevant form of the question, or failure to
record or code information fully, results in inadequate
material for primary or secondary analysis. In this last
category we find both variables which should be easy to
deal with (such as age and the 'ethnicity' variables) and
others which pose more far-reaching problems (such as
education and occupation).

XII Interviewer Comments

Although not directly related to standardization, interviewer comments deserve a few remarks in this context. It is a widespread practice to have each interviewer jot down, at the end of each schedule, comments about problems or conditions during the interview. As far as one can tell from code books and coding manuals, little systematic use is made of these materials.

A great deal of interesting information, much of it relevant to standardization, could be collected in this way if survey agencies were to code it on each respondent's file or on some separate log. For example, although the questionnaires may be written in only one or two languages, interviews may be conducted in several languages, the interviewer or a third party (such as another member of the family or a neighbour) acting as interpreter. Both the method of translation and the language should be noted, together with any questions which proved particularly difficult or ambiguous in translation. For certain research topics, particularly sensitive ones, it may be useful to have some evaluation of the respondent's receptivity or hostility as the case may be. Likewise it may be relevant to know if the interview has taken place with other people present, or if there have been interruptions. In using untested questions, interviewers may usefully be asked to note difficulties encountered with particular techniques, and so on.

Generally such comments should take the form of specific and preferably pre-coded questions to the interviewer to ensure that the type of information provided is comprehensive and to the point. A number of established survey organizations adopt this practice quite regularly. However, feedback from interviewers could be more systematically encouraged both by these and other means (such as the use of tape recorders and investigator participation with professional interviewers in pretests).

One important use of secondary analysis of surveys involves the evaluation of methods of data collection and coding. Such analysis forms the basis for refining measurements for future studies. In this light it is reasonable to think of existing data sets as pretests for future research instruments. As in any pretest, great weight must be placed on interviewers' opinions of the effectiveness of particular questions and techniques (although other considerations are also crucial). We therefore urge scholars to make more use of such comments, and we recommend that they be recorded or summarized in some accessible form.

XIII Conclusions and Recommendations

This report has dealt with two interrelated but distinct aspects of survey research, standardization of data and possibilities for secondary analysis. These concluding remarks will also try to cover both aspects. To the degree we find — or can impose — standardized questions and coding schemes, we also enhance the value of secondary analysis. But the latter activity is much broader in scope and intent than standardization, which is simply a prerequisite. Important as standardization is, it must be evaluated in terms of its contribution to analysis. We have tried to keep this in mind, and this assumption underlies the repeated reference to clusters of variables which may be viewed as, at least partially, interchangeable. The substitutability of variables, for certain limited purposes, in no way eliminates the need to achieve uniformity on any given variable, nor does it reduce the difficulties; but it can enable scholars to make more extensive use of existing data sets even though each is imperfect in many respects.

The following remarks are stated unequivocally, in order to highlight the points. We trust that readers will recall the relevant qualifications we have interjected throughout the text.

1)The process of standardization is already under way among Canadian social surveys. We have seen that many of the most commonly used socio-demographic variables (age, education, occupation, language, and others) appear in nearly all surveys examined here. Furthermore, there is a suprising degree of uniformity considering the notorious 'individualism' of academic researchers. One should not belittle the difficulties remaining in the way of standardization, especially for occupation, education, and ethnicity; but the situation is definitely not hopeless.

2)Standardization must be conceived in terms of coded responses and not simply in terms of question wording. Respondents interpret similar questions in different ways, construe different questions in similar ways, and fail to respond to certain questions. All such variation is reflected in the coded responses, which after all are what scholars actually analyze. While it is, therefore, useful to experiment with different questions, and with non-verbal forms of eliciting responses such as card-sorts, one must continually ask about the payoff in terms of a)more information, b)better information (more precise, more useable form), and c)comparability with other information.

This is not an argument that no attention should be given to exact wording; rather we need to know whether divergent methods yield the coded data we want. The purposes to which data are put therefore remain a central concern. In too many cases, one suspects, an investigator does not consider how minor changes of procedure could enhance the value of his data for other scholars or for himself. Omnibus variables may not be practical, but those serving a variety of purposes should be devised and used wherever possible.

3)False economics account for much of the current lack of standardization. In particular, investigators fail to code the information they collect in a substantial proportion of cases. Failure to ask certain 'basic' questions like ethnicity or occupation also 'costs' the scholarly community while saving only a small amount of time and money in any one survey.

Investigators cannot, of course, bear these costs personally, but granting agencies will undoubtedly see the great marginal utility of these added costs in terms of secondary analysis. At present the burden of encouraging researchers to include basic questions they personally do not intend to use falls only too frequently on the survey agencies involved at great cost to them in direct expenditure (not charging for the additional questions or coding involved) or lost contracts due to higher bids.

4)Social theories and standardized data form mutually reinforcing bases for research. At several points we have noted how helpful a theory (even untested) would be for guiding one's judgments about category boundaries or variable substitution. Similarly, as uniformity of practice allows the study of time series, comparative studies, and merging of data sets (for sub-group analysis with adequate Ns), we should see the more rapid growth of theory, because adequate tests become feasible and less expensive (since one does not need to collect the data afresh each time).

5)One should never collect new data until one has examined existing data sets to see if they will serve one's purpose. Quite often, of course, new data must be sought, especially when new theories are propounded. But the exercise of secondary analysis, even when it reveals a blind alley, will frequently serve to improve the quality of the new data subsequently collected. If nothing else, canvassing the available code books and questionnaires highlights question wording, formats, and methods which the scholar may not have known or which he had no prior basis for evaluating. This report, it is hoped, will serve a similar purpose.

6)Respondents should not be relied on to standardize responses. The 'job' of the respondent is to answer questions as fully and accurately as possible within ethical constraints and within his own understanding and level of articulateness. When respondents agree on stereotyped answers, we should re-examine our questions. Standardization is necessary and is a problem precisely to the extent that we are successful in eliciting rich responses.

7)Interviewers should not be relied on, more than absolutely necessary, to standardize responses. The 'job' of the interviewer is to capture as fully and accurately as possible the statements and nuances of responses. To expect an interviewer simultaneously to standardize those responses will often lead to distortion. Of course, pre-coded questions allow (indeed force) the interviewers to fit responses to existing categories; but we should only use categories that are well defined and easily applied. At the same time, interviewers must have instructions about potential coding problems (e.g., 'engineer') so that they can spot responses requiring follow-up. But it is, even then, not their job to code these.

8)Standardization can be achieved fully only after analysis begins. Although comparable questions and elaborate coding schemes aid standardization, there is no substitute for a scholar's 'feel' for the data. Knowing that some provinces require only grade 11, some grade 12, and some grade 13 for college entrance is the scholar's responsibility and will not generally be built into a coding scheme of years of formal schooling. Similarly, cost of living changes will necessitate adjustment of upper boundaries for income comparisons over time, although it is generally not feasible to build these in when coding is originally done. (Machine re-coding could, of course, take account of these changes by adjusting scores to reflect 'constant dollars' in 1960 and 1970 or whatever.)

9)Standardization should be based on professional norms. It is, therefore, not eternal but changes as our understanding evolves and as our techniques improve. The presence or absence of a norm is often masked by the apparently natural orderliness of the subject matter. For example, we saw that 'age' was quite standardized in survey research. It might appear that this is solely because it is a simpler phenomenon than 'occupation' or 'ethnicity.' But the increasing interest in aging processes, and the more frequent use of cohort analysis, makes plain the value of a developing norm about coding exact age or, preferably, date of birth. If one were concerned to test astrological theories (as someone will eventually), we will find that 'age' is not a matter of coding year of birth, but month, day, and hour of birth. Age means different things in different theories, and therefore standardized forms will vary as our theories and degree of understanding change.

10)The recommendations we have made are intended as 'default options.' That is, while we do not adhere to any rigid creed based on prior wisdom, we do believe that scholars will benefit from at least knowing what models have been evolved and tested by others; unless they are disposed to give serious thought to alternatives, they are more likely to avoid pitfalls by falling back on tried techniques than by indulging in improvisation.

XIV Studies Examined for the Report

Below are listed the survey studies which we examined for this report. From the comprehensiveness of the list, readers may judge for themselves the extent to which the results we have presented may be generalized. The list may also remind scholars of existing studies in fields of interest to them.

In the following list, we have tried to include information on:

1)title of study (not necessarily the 'official' title, but a descriptive one) and the languages in which interviews were conducted;

2)principal investigator; university affiliation, if any;

3)year in which interviews were conducted; and

4)geographic extent of sample.

Despite our best efforts, it proved impossible, in many cases, to obtain all of these items of information. We have relied primarily on published code books, where they exist, and wherever possible we have consulted the original questionnaire and supplementary materials (such as coding manuals). We apologize for incorrect or incomplete information, but it was impossible to be more precise or accurate in many cases, given the extent and quality of available documentation and the time available to us. A topic partly beyond our scope, but requiring attention (from data banks and from funding agencies), is the problem of the standardization of code books and general documentation.

The languages listed need explanation. There are often two such languages; the first we mention is that in which the majority of the fieldwork was conducted. Documentation on studies was collected by us in two batches, one comprising studies originating mainly in Quebec and initiated by researchers in that province; the other comprising studies originating elsewhere in Canada and initiated by investigators in other provinces. The former have been referred to in the text as 'French-language studies,' and the latter as 'English-language studies.' It should be noted, however, that there is some overlap between the two, since studies originating in Quebec may well be conducted mostly in English, depending on the population sampled. This ambiguity applies also to national studies which comprise interviews in several languages. Thus too much weight should not be given to fine distinctions between

'French' and 'English' studies; tabulations have been presented separately to give an idea of broad trends in the two language communities.

It should be observed that the total number of studies appearing in the tabulations is often greater than the number of studies listed. This is because several studies included more than one research instrument, because of different target populations (e.g., students and teachers) and different waves. When the different instruments showed substantial differences in terms of socio-economic material included, they were analyzed as separate studies.

Most studies are listed under the name of the principal investigator, where applicable, or under that of the survey organization which designed and conducted them. Where we have been unable to obtain the above information, we have listed either the funding agency or (more commonly) the organization which carried out the fieldwork. We do not wish to slight any of the persons involved in these studies; our main purpose in listing specific individuals or institutions was to provide information to prospective investigators about whom to contact to obtain further information about a study or permission for secondary analysis of it.

Alberta 71 Project (English) (Title and languages)
Richard Baird, University of Alberta (Principal investigator)
1971 (Year)
Provincial (Geographic extent)

Study of Career Decisions of Canadian Youth (English, French)
(teacher questionnaire)
Raymond Breton, University of Toronto
1965
National

Study of Career Decisions of Canadian Youth (English, French)
(student questionnaire)
Raymond Breton, University of Toronto
1965
National

Gallup Poll (English, French)[44]
Gallup Poll
1968
National

Draft Questionnaire for 1972 Federal Election Study (English)
Directed by John Meisel and others (CPSA committee)
1972
National

Edmonton Centre Election Study (English)
University of Alberta, Department of Political Science
1968
Constituency

Survey of West End Residents for Marathon Realty (English)
Forbes, Goldberg, and Kelly, University of British Columbia
1970
Vancouver

*A Survey of Canadian Attitudes toward the Federal Government and
Its Information Services* (English, French)
Canadian Facts, Ltd.
1968
National

Time Budgets (English)
George Gray, University of British Columbia
1971
Vancouver

Student Opinion Survey (English, French)
Ted Harvey and N. Chi
Unknown
International

Social and Political Attitudes in Ontario (English)
David Hoffman and Fred Schindeler, York University
1968
Ontario

Vancouver Burrard, 1963 Federal Election (English)
Jean Laponce, University of British Columbia
1963
Constituency

Vancouver Burrard, 1965 Federal Election (English)
Jean Laponce, University of British Columbia
1965
Constituency

Japanese in Lethbridge, Alberta (English)
Unknown
Unknown
Lethbridge

Left-Right Survey (English)
Jean Laponce, University of British Columbia
1968
International

Left-Right Hand Survey (English)
Jean Laponce, University of British Columbia
1970
Sub-provincial region, B.C.

Questionnaire Survey (English)
Jean Laponce, University of British Columbia
1974
Institution (U.B.C.)

1965 Canadian National Election Study (English, French)
Philip Converse, University of Michigan
John Meisel, Queen's University
Maurice Pinard, McGill University
Peter Regenstreif, University of Rochester
Mildred Schwartz, University of Illinois
1966
National

1968 Canadian National Election Study (English, French)
John Meisel, Queen's University
1968
National

Opinion Survey of Canadian Youth (English, French)
Canadian Facts Limited and National Opinion Research Centre
1965
National

Occupational Expectations Questionnaire (English)
Faculty of Commerce and Business Administration, University of
British Columbia
Unknown
Institution (U.B.C.)

Real Estate 'Wab' Study (English)
Unknown
1973
Vancouver

Public Opinion Questionnaire (English, French)
John Sinclair, University of Alberta
S.I. Pobihushchy, University of New Brunswick
1969
National

Socio-Economic Survey of Vancouver Island (English)
C. Verner and G. Dickinson, University of British Columbia
1969
Sub-provincial region

Housing and Social Integration of Immigrants (several languages)
Anthony Richmond, York University
1969
Toronto

1967 Election Study (English)
New Democratic Party of Ontario
1967
Provincial

Opinion of Residents on Medical Services in Ontario (English, French)
Survey Research Centre, York University
1972
Provincial

Survey on Neighbourhood Opinions and Attitudes (English)
Anthony Richmond, York University
1968
Toronto

Part-time Degree Students Survey (English)
Survey Research Centre, York University
Institute for the Quantitative Analysis of Social and Economic Policy,
University of Toronto
1971
Ontario

Waterloo South By-Election (English)
J.M. Wilson, University of Waterloo
1964
Constituency

Multi-National Student Survey (several languages)
Western Behavioural Sciences Institute
1969
International

Agger Five Community (English)
Robert Agger, McMaster University
Unknown
International

Highly Qualified Manpower Survey (English, French)
Statistics Canada
1973
National

1971 Census of Canada (English, French)
Statistics Canada
1971
National

Job Mobility Survey (English, French)
Statistics Canada
1973
National

A Study of Educational Plans of Ontario High School Students
(English)
Survey Research Centre, York University

Unknown
Provincial

Manitoba Electorate Study (English)
J.M. Wilson, University of Waterloo
1973
Provincial

Alberta Electorate Study (English)
University of Lethbridge, University of Alberta
1970
Provincial

The Modern Life and Health Survey (English)
University of Alberta
1970
Provincial

Study of Career Decisions of Secondary School Teachers (English)
Sociology Department, Carleton University
1973
Provincial

Study of Career Orientation and Political Behaviour of Undergraduate Students (English)
Graduate Students, Carleton University
1970
Institution (Carleton)

Neighbourhood and Population Movement (small questionnaire)
Survey Research Centre, York University
1969
Toronto

Neighbourhoods and Population Movement (large questionnaire)
(English)
Survey Research Centre, York University
1969
Toronto

Basic Background Items for U.S. Household Surveys (English)
Roxann Van Dusen and Nicholas Zill
Social Science Research Council, Washington, D.C.
1975
Standardization of variables

Exercice de la profession de pharmacien au Canada (English, French)
Edward Harvey
1969
Large Canadian cities

Utilisation des drogues à des fins non médicales (English, French)
Sondra Phillips
1970
National

Etudiants étrangers au Canada (English, French)
Jacques Dofny, University of Montreal
1970
Twenty Canadian universities

Etude électorale provinciale (French, English)
Serge Carlos and Daniel Latouche
1970
Montreal

Usage des langues dans le monde du travail au Québec (French,
English)
Centre for Survey Research, University of Montreal
1971
Provincial

Réaction sociale à la déviance (French, English)
François-Xavier Ribordy
1971
Montreal and Toronto

Etude sur les mouvements sociaux (French, English)
Maurice Pinard, McGill University
1970
Quebec

Associations des partis fédéraux (English, French)
Sheilagh Koeppen
1973
Canada — Federal party executives

Fécondité de la femme au Québec (French, English)
Jacques Henripin, University of Montreal
1971
Quebec

Migration à l'Ile des Soeurs (French, English)
Bryn Greer-Wootten
1971
Residents of Ile des Soeurs, Montreal

Etude de quatre zones résidentielles de Montréal (French)
Marie Lavigne
1972
Four neighbourhoods in central Montreal

Aspirations scolaires et orientations professionnelles étudiantes
(French, English)
Guy Rocher and Pierre W. Bélanger
1972
Students, parents, teachers and principals — Quebec

Services offerts aux étudiants (French)
Centre for Survey Research, University of Montreal
1972
University of Montreal students

Le loisir en milieu urbain (French)
Roger Levasseur and Gilles Pronovost
1972
Ste-Foy and Trois-Rivières

Sports et socialisation (English, French)
Gerald Kenyon
1973
Montreal and Toronto

Langues non officielles (English, French and others)
Kenneth O'Bryan
1973
Large Canadian cities (Montreal, Toronto, Winnipeg, Edmonton, Vancouver, Halifax)

Formation professionelle des adultes et mobilité de la main d'oeuvre (French)
Jean Primeau
1972
Quebec – Canadian Association For Adult Education

Réseau de communications dans la famille (French)
Colette Carisse
1972
Montreal

Mobilité résidentielle dans neuf quartiers de Montréal (French, English)
Bryn Greer-Wootten
1972
Nine Montreal neighbourhoods

Participation à la culture populaire (French, English)
Centre for Survey Research, University of Montreal
1973
A Quebec city and a Montreal neighbourhood. An Ontario city and a Toronto neighbourhood

Recherche sur les diplômés en droit (French, English)
André Lajoie and Claude Parizeau
1973
Law graduates of Quebec universities and the University of Ottawa

Elections scolaires 1973 (1) (French, English)
Centre for Survey Research, University of Montreal
1973
Montreal

Elections scolaires 1973 (2) (French, English)
Centre for Survey Research, University of Montreal
1973
Montreal

Communications (French)
James Taylor
1973
Montreal and Ste-Marie de Beauce

Humanistes (English, French)
Centre for Survey Research, University of Montreal
1974
Professors working in the 'humanities' in some 30 Canadian universities

Sentiments religieux des Québécois (French)
Centre for Survey Research, University of Montreal
1973
Quebec

Mobilité forcée (French)
Marie Lavigne
1974
Montreal centre

La tâche des enseignants du collégial (French, English)
Centre for Survey Research, University of Montreal
1974
CEGEP teachers, Province of Quebec

Inadaptation juvénile (French, English)
Marc Leblanc
1974
Montreal secondary school students

Recherche sur la formation juridique (French, English)
Andrée Lajoie and Claude Parizeau
1974
Law students in Quebec universities and the University of Ottawa

Satisfaction des étudiants de l'éducation permanente (French)
Centre for Survey Research, University of Montreal
1974
University of Montreal

Satisfaction des clients de C. I. C.
Centre for Survey Research, University of Montreal
1974
Montreal

Participation politique et sociale (French)
Diane Bernier and Paul Valois
1974
Montreal

Conditionnement physique des Québécois (French, English)
Centre for Survey Research, University of Montreal
1974
Province of Quebec

Rôle de l'ombudsman au Québec (French, English)
Centre for Survey Research, University of Montreal
1974
Province of Quebec

Enquête auprès des résidents de l'Ile de Hull (French)
Caroline Andrew and André Blais
1974
Hull, Quebec

Recherche sur l'institut provincial des sports (French)
Centre for Survey Research, University of Montreal
1974
Province of Quebec

Recherche auprès des membres de la Caisse Populaire de Cartierville
(French)
Centre for Survey Research, University of Montreal
1974
Cartierville (Montreal)

Attitudes des groupes majoritaires (English, French)
J.W. Berry, R. Kalin, D. Taylor
1974
Canada

Accidents et maladies de travail (English, French)
Social development centre
1974
Province of Quebec

Rôle des comités d'école (French, English)
Centre for Survey Research, University of Montreal
1974
Montreal

Education des groupes populaires (French)
Gisèle Legault
1974
Montreal

Médicaments brevetés (English, French)
Health and welfare departments
1974
Two Ontario cities, Montreal, New Brunswick

Etude politique (French, English)
Social research group
1962
Province of Quebec

L'alcool chez les jeunes québécois (French)
E.A. Faltah, Cécile Goudreau-Toutant, R. Tremblay
1968
Montreal

Ingénieurs canadiens-français et canadiens-anglais (French, English)
Jacques Dofny, University of Montreal
1967 (?)
Montreal

Etude élection provinciale 1973 (French, English)
Richard Hamilton and Maurice Pinard
1973
Province of Quebec

Etude élection fédérale (French, English)
Richard Hamilton and Maurice Pinard
1972
Province of Quebec

Etude électorale 1960 (French, English)
Social research group
1960
Province of Quebec

Enseignement de la religion dans les écoles (French)
Social research group
1964
Eight Quebec cities

Effets de la télévision (French)
Social research group
1963-64
Sherbrooke, Joliette, Chicoutimi

Séparatisme (French)
Social research group
1963
Province of Quebec

Satisfaction au travail (English, French)
Social research group
1963-64
CN workers in seven large Canadian cities

Relations interethniques (English, French)
Social research group
1965
Canada

Schisme créditiste (French)
Maurice Pinard
1973
Province of Quebec

Etudes sur les élites industrielles au Québec (English, French)
Arnaud Sales
1974
Province of Quebec

Orientations professionnelles (French)
Social research group
1962
Montreal — secondary schools

Etude des consommateurs (French, English)
Social research group
1964
Montreal

Choix occupationnels (English, French)
Social research group
1964
Eight Canadian cities

Conditions sociales de l'enseignement (French)
Social research group
1962
Members of the Catholic professors' alliance, Montreal

Relations canado-américaines (English, French)
Social research group
1964
Canada

Etude de la justice (French)
Department of Criminology, University of Montreal
Unknown
Province of Quebec

Recherche sur les droits de l'homme (French)
Denis Szabo, University of Montreal
1968
Province of Quebec

Attitudes envers la sexualité (French)
Department of Criminology, University of Montreal
1970
Montreal

Relations entre la police et le public (French, English)
Department of Criminology, University of Montreal
Unknown
Montreal

Recherche sur les partis politiques au Québec (1) (French, English)
Vincent Lemieux
1968 to 1970
Province of Quebec

Recherche sur les partis politiques au Québec (2) (French, English)
Vincent Lemieux
1968 to 1970
Province of Quebec

Recherche sur les partis politiques au Québec (3) (French, English)
Vincent Lemieux
1968 to 1970
Province of Quebec

Sondage pré-électoral – élections provinciales 1970 (1) (French, English)
Vincent Lemieux and Marcel Gilbert
1970
Province of Quebec

Sondages pré-électoral – élections provinciales 1970 (French, English)
Vincent Lemieux
1970
Province of Quebec

Sondage pré-électoral dans le comté de Lévis – 1970 (French, English)
Vincent Lemieux
1970
Electors of Lévis county, Quebec

Sondage pré-électoral – élections provinciales 1973 (French, English)
André Blais, Vincent Lemieux, François Renaud
1973
Province of Quebec

La vie municipale à Laval (French)
André Ouellet
1969
Ville de Laval, Quebec

Attitudes envers les partis politiques (French)
Vincent Lemieux
1968-69
Two Quebec counties

Recherche sur la communauté universitaire (French)
Louise Ouellet
1972
Laval University students

Options constitutionnelles des enseignants (French)
Vincent Lemieux
1968
Quebec teachers

XV Notes

1. The words 'question,' 'variable,' 'item,' and 'observation' are used interchangeably in this report, except where the context makes clear a distinction between them. Occasionally, 'response' is used in a manner similar to observation, but the context again should clarify this usage.

2. For a preliminary effort at standardization in the United States, see *Basic Background Items for U.S. Household Surveys: Draft Report of the SSRC Working Group on the Standardization of Survey Background Items*, June 1974, mimeo. For information, contact Nicholas Zill, SSRC, 1755 Massachusetts Avenue, N.W., Washington, D.C., 20036, U.S.A. For preliminary work in Britain, see Margaret Stacey, ed., *Comparability in Social Research* (London: Heinemann Educational Books, 1969).

3. See, for example, Adam Przeworski and Henry Teune, *The Logic of Comparative Social Inquiry* (N.Y.: Wiley, 1970); Robert Holt and John Turner, eds., *The Methodology of Comparative Research* (N.Y.: Free Press, 1970), relevant issues of *International Social Science Journal* and the *Public Opinion Quarterly*, among others.

4. We applied these general criteria to studies currently available through major data banks, such as those of York University, Centre de Sondage at the University of Montreal, and University of British Columbia, and through major published reports of Statistics Canada.

5. A certain degree of standardization has been achieved through uniformity of practice within major survey organizations on question wording and coding. Standardization is not as complete as might be expected, however, in that these organizations are not always responsible for the design of research instruments they are called upon to administer. Also much remains to be done in standardization between organizations, and it is hoped that this report will lead to steps in this direction.

6. In some cases, sponsoring agencies may prohibit certain questions, or specify categories they deem important but which have little re-use potential. This problem seems most likely to occur in contract research.

7. 'Cost' may, in some cases, take the form of computing time or programming skills. Where an investigator must rely on simple, hand tabulations, there is some justification for few categories. Given the availability of standard statistical packages, however, this should provide little justification in the future.

8. 'French' and 'English,' in this context, refer to the language of the questionnaire we used for our analysis; they do not refer only to studies done solely in one or the other language. See the detailed explanation at the end of this report where we list all the studies consulted.

9. Since all of the telephone surveys in our report were done primarily in French, we cannot be certain about the 'independent variable' here. It seems likely, however, that the factors connected with telephone surveys, noted below, account for the differences in Table 4.

10. That a degree of consensus exists on certain variables can be a source of danger as well as a help to scholars. The dangers are that we may take for granted the meaning of the variables, and that we may also assume we understand the causal or explanatory status of the variables. As an example of the first danger, consider age: when we 'control' for age and find systematic differences between groups in a 'dependent' variable, is this a result of aging or of generation? As control variables, any of the variables in this report may exemplify the dangers of imparting causal status, as analyzed by Paul Meehl, 'Nuisance Variables and the Ex Post Facto Design,' *Minnesota Studies in the Philosophy of Science*, Vol. IV, ed. Michael Radner and Stephen Winokur (University of Minnesota Press, 1970), pp. 373-402. This chapter is essential background for any sophisticated use of sociodemographic characteristics as 'controls' or 'matching' variables.

11. The wording may be adapted to elicit this information about someone other than the respondent.

12. Common law marriage and 'religious marriage' can have separate categories, if desired.

13. Both forms of the question may be adapted for different persons or time periods.

14. When asking about residence as a child, one must specify an age or age-range, since many people in Canada have lived in communities of different size at different ages. An ambiguity which we have not fully resolved concerns whether the respondent, referring to residence as a child, indicates size of the community then or its size now. For most purposes this is not a serious problem but some towns have grown very rapidly; and some very old respondents may refer to communities as they were 50 or more years ago. Ascertaining the name of the town or area might be the best approach.

15. This should be supplemented by a precise geographical location, wherever feasible, such as enumeration area, census tract number, or electoral riding (or all three).

16. If possible, these responses should be broken down into city centre and suburbs.

17. In personal interviews, it is probably simplest to use a flashcard rather than read out all of these responses.

18. Childhood may be defined in terms of other age ranges, but this should be clear from the question. If a respondent has lived in

several places of different size during childhood, these may be coded separately with only a few additional columns.

19. Although we recommend ascertaining number of moves in lifetime, number in past five years has considerable attraction since that is what Statistics Canada generally asks. This question can obviously be followed up by asking about other members of household (e.g., head, if respondent is not head), or about other time periods (e.g., asking first about lifetime moves and then about more recent ones).

20. Other time periods could be used, but we recommend six months.

21. Statistics Canada, *Interviewer's Manual: The Labour Force Survey* (March 1974), section 3, page 1.

22. If theoretical interests dictate, one may ask about family rather than household. Obviously, neither is relevant in certain types of institutional samples.

23. Several satisfactory alternative forms of this question should be noted:
    1)'How many children do you have (still living)?'
    2)'How many children have you had altogether (all children born alive)?'
    3)(Statistics Canada question for women only) 'How many babies have you had, not counting stillbirths?'
    4)'How many children do you have, including any you may have adopted?'

24. In addition, clear and comprehensive instructions must be given to interviewers so they know whom to include in the list. For example, what constitutes 'usual place of residence' for students at boarding schools? Likewise coders must have exhaustive criteria for classifications, since they (not interviewers) will presumably group household members into relevant categories.

25. Of course, one may use these variables without concern for the ways in which they indicate social status. For example, one may wish to identify farmers or businessmen to study role sets and correlated attitudes; then one obviously cannot substitute a measure of education or class. Our hunch, however, is that these variables are most frequently used as background or 'control' variables indicating status. If so, they are frequently adequate (although not ideal) substitutes for each other.

26. Bernard Blishen, 'The Construction and Use of an Occupational Class Scale,' *Canadian Journal of Economics and Political Science*, 24 (Nov. 1958), 519-31; and Blishen, 'Socio-Economic Index for Occupation in Canada,' *Canadian Review of Sociology and Anthropology*, 4 (1967), 41-53.

27. Roger Lapierre, *Systèmes de classification des occupations*, (M.Sc. thesis, University of Montreal, 1974).

28. The occupation question alone may be used for past situations, e.g., first job: 'What type of work did you do at your first job?'; or father's occupation: 'What type of work did your father do for most of his active life?' or 'What type of work was your father doing when you were about 18 years old (or, if he was deceased, what type of work did he do for most of his active life)?'

29. Interviewer should be instructed to probe as necessary for exact description of work done, and warned of possible ambiguous job titles, e.g., 'engineer,' 'contractor,' 'operator.' Use of 'sector of employment' question as a supplement to occupation will help eliminate some such ambiguities.

30. Recall the discussion above of the crucial distinction between household and family. Since there are excellent theoretical reasons for focusing on one rather than the other, this choice (and the definition used by interviewers) must be included prominently in the code book or other documentation.

31. That is, the letters are not in alphabetical order according to level of income; 'A' does not equal lowest income level, or highest.

32. If 'family' income is the focus, a slightly different follow-up question may be necessary.

33. Special sub-populations such as students or business executives will require different categories. Most students earn under $5000 a year, so finer breakdowns may be advisable in that range. These can always be collapsed by other users of the data, and hence pose no problem. One study of high-level business executives had a category of 'under $40,000,' several intermediate ones, and a top category of '$300,000 and over.' What can we say?

34. For example, see the article by Peter C. Pineo and John C. Goyder, 'Social Class Identification of National Sub-Groups,' in *Social Stratification: Canada*, ed. J.E. Curtis and W.G. Scott (Scarborough: Prentice-Hall of Canada, 1973).

35. Mildred Schwartz, 'Canadian Voting Behaviour,' in *Electoral Behavior: A Comparative Reader*, ed. Richard Rose (N.Y.: Free Press, 1974); and N.B. Ryder, 'The Interpretation of Origin Statistics,' *Canadian Journal of Economics and Political Science*, 21 (Nov. 1955), 466-79.

36. Frequently encountered variants ask 'What is your religious preference?' or 'What religion do you feel closest to, even if you do not practice?' These may also be used as follow-up questions for those who declare no religion.
Complexity of coding scheme and therefore number of columns will vary according to religious heterogeneity of population sampled. The above code is used nationally by Statistics Canada. As ethnic indicators other religions may usefully be added in re-

gions where numbers warrant it: Russian Orthodox, Ukrainian Orthodox, Buddhist, Muslim, Hindu, etc.

37. 'Mother tongue' has been defined by Statistics Canada as the language first learned and still understood (even though it may not be used as frequently as other languages currently). See, Statistics Canada, 1971 Census of Canada, *Content Manual*, p. 25; and *Census Questions and Answers*, p. 46.

38. For general use in national surveys, the following categories should be sufficient; but for provincial or local samples, more or fewer categories may be needed depending on the linguistic heterogeneity and composition of the population.

39. Ethnic origin, according to the definition used by the Census, refers to descent on the male side. 'Ethnic or cultural group refers to descent (through the father's side) and should not be confused with citizenship....Use as guide if applicable in your case: 1)The language you spoke on first coming to this continent, if you were born outside of Canada. 2)If born in Canada, the language spoken by your ancestor on the male side when he came here.' Statistics Canada, 1971 Census, *Content Manual*, p. 72.

40. If theoretical interests justify it, this may be asked twice — once for father's side and again for mother's side. The form suggested here, however, has the advantage of conforming to Statistics Canada practice.

41. In some provinces and localities, this should be broken down into English, Scottish and Welsh.

42. For a recent discussion, see P.M. Sniderman, et al., 'Party Loyalty and Electoral Volatility: A Study of the Canadian Party System,' *Canadian Journal of Political Science*, 7 (June 1974), 268-88, and the references cited there.

43. Generally it will not be appropriate to rephrase these questions to elicit information about persons other than the respondent, since spouse, children, friends, etc., will not generally know details about offices held or number of hours worked.

44. We included only one example of a Gallup (C.I.P.O.) questionnaire, since a quick examination of them, over a 20-year period, revealed only minor variation in variables included and in question wording and coding. We also examined an example (1970) of work by the Public Opinion Research Centre, Montreal.